Indian Views
OF THE
Custer Fight

INDIAN VIEWS

of the

CUSTER FIGHT

a source book

compiled and edited by
RICHARD G. HARDORFF

UNIVERSITY OF OKLAHOMA PRESS
Norman

Also by Richard G. Hardorff:

The Oglala Lakota Crazy Horse: A preliminary Study and Annotated Listing of Primary Sources (Mattituck, NY, 1985)

Markers, Artifacts and Indian Testimony: Preliminary Findings on the Custer Battle (Short Hills, NJ, 1985)

The Custer Battle Casualties: Burials, Exhumations and Reinterments (El Segundo, CA, 1989)

Lakota Recollections of the Custer Fight: New Sources of Indian-Military History (Spokane, WA, 1991)

Hokahey! A Good Day to Die! The Indian Casualties of the Custer Fight (Spokane, WA, 1993)

Cheyenne Memories of the Custer Fight: A Sourcebook (Spokane, WA, 1995)

Camp, Custer, and the Little Bighorn: A Collection of Walter Mason Camp's Research Papers on General Custer's Last Fight (El Segundo, CA, 1997)

The Surrender and Death of Crazy Horse: A Sourcebook on a Tragic Episode in Lakota History (Spokane, WA, 1998)

The Custer Battle Casualties, II: The Dead, The Missing, and A Few Survivors (El Segundo, CA, 1998)

On the Little Bighorn with Walter Camp (El Segundo, CA, 2000)

Walter M. Camp's Little Bighorn Rosters (Spokane, WA, 2002)

Library of Congress Cataloging-in-Publication Data

Indian views of the Custer fight : a source book / compiled and edited by Richard G. Hardorff.
    p. cm.
Includes bibliographical references and index.
ISBN 0-8061-3690-1
1. Little Bighorn, Battle of the, Mont., 1876--Personal narratives.
2. Cheyenne Indians--Wars, 1876. 3. Cheyenne
Indians--History--Sources. 4. Dakota Indians--Wars, 1876. 5. Dakota
Indians--History--Sources. I. Hardorff, Richard G. II. Series.
E83.876.I53 2003
973.8'2--dc21

                    2003001296

Originally published by the Arthur H. Clark Company copyright © 2004 by Richard G. Hardoff. Paperback edition published 2005 by the University of Oklahoma Press, Norman, Publishing Division of the University. All rights reserved. Manufactured in the U.S.A.

                    2 3 4 5 6 7 8 9 10

To
MEISJE and RENÉE
with fond memories

Contents

Maps

Introduction

This is the third and final volume of Indian testimony about the Battle of the Little Bighorn compiled by the author. More commonly known as Custer's Last Stand, it resulted in the disastrous retreat of Major Marcus A. Reno's battalion and the subsequent annihilation of five companies commanded by General George A. Custer, on June 25, 1876. On the following day the Indians resumed the battle with the remainder of the regiment, inflicting heavy casualties on the entrenched troops. The victors abandoned the battlefield on June 27 upon the arrival of a military relief column.

Like its companion volumes *Lakota Recollections* and *Cheyenne Memories*, the present volume contains the observations of Sioux and Cheyenne Indians who were eyewitnesses to the fight. These observations were extracted from letters, newspaper accounts, Army reports, and manuscripts. The reader should be aware that the quoted statements contained in these sources are English renditions of the Sioux and the Cheyenne languages, and that these translations may have been subject to distortion.

The recorded statements obtained from Indian combatants were actually the end product of a filtering process which often involved the interaction of three individuals: a narrator, a translator, and an interviewer. More often than not, these combined efforts were marred by the distortions of the narrator, the improficiencies of the interpreter, and the lack of objectivity of the interviewer.

Indian testimony was usually discounted by scholars because of its apparent conflict with the known facts and established theories. Fear of reprisals may account for some of these distortions, which was apparent in some of their early statements. There also existed a general misunderstanding of the Indian culture in which embellishment of one's prowess was a socially accepted practice. In addition to these factors, Indian recollections were also subject to unintentional forgetfulness caused by the passage of time.

Despite these weaknesses, the Indian statements contained in the present volume and the two preceding ones fill a void in our limited knowledge of Custer's battle. The details in these statements offer new perspectives on the movements of the cavalry and the Indian force on the battlefield. In addition, their statements are often deeply personal in the disclosure of tragedies and triumphs. Lastly, they reveal battle incidents which no other source could provide.

Indian Views presents the much-neglected Indian side of the Custer story as told through the views of twenty-nine Sioux and nine Cheyennes. Their statements were obtained by Army personnel, newspaper correspondents, anthropologists, historians, and others who were genuinely interested in our frontier. The prologue and epilogue contain the impressions of three Seventh Cavalry soldiers, while the appendix presents Walter M. Camp's analytical conclusions of General Terry's order to Custer. Their combined efforts resulted in a valuable contribution to the historiography of one of the most dramatic and controversial episodes in our military history. It is hoped that the publication of this corpus of text will lead to new perspectives on the battle.

The author is indebted to many individuals who assisted with this volume. The following were especially helpful. Barbara Dey, Reference Librarian at the Colorado Historical Society, Denver, for her assistance with the George Bent Manuscript Collection; Eleanor M. Gehres, Western History Manager, Denver Public Library, for her assistance with the Charles White Diary housed in the Robert Ellison Collection; Kitty Deernose, Special Collections, Little Bighorn Battlefield National Monument, NPS, for her assistance with the Walter M. Camp Collection; Bradford Koplowitz, Assistant Curator, University of Oklahoma Library at Norman, for his assistance with the Stanley Campbell Collection; John M. Cahoon, Collections Manager, Seaver Center, Los Angeles, for his assistance with the Curtis Manuscript; Bob Knecht, Assistant Manuscripts Curator, Kansas State Historical Society at Topeka, for his assistance with the Joseph G. Masters Collection; Dr. Bonnie Hardwick, Curator, Bancroft Library, Berkeley, California, for her assistance with the Oscar F. Long Papers; Brad Westwood, Assistant Curator, Harold B. Lee Library, Provo, Utah, for assistance with the Special Collections; and, lastly, Dr. James S. Brust, San Pedro, California, Bruce R. Liddic, Syracuse, New York, and Tom O'Neil, Brooklyn, New York, for sharing documents with me which were of special interest to this publication.

Genoa, Illinois   Richard G. Hardorff
February 9, 2002

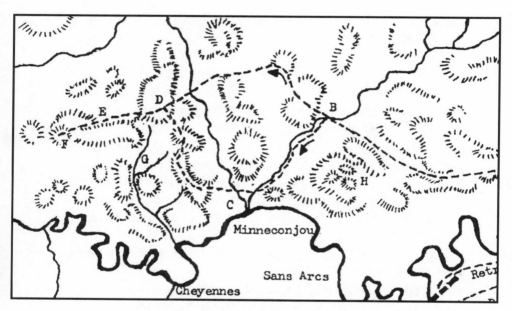

THE LITTLE BIGHORN BATTLEFIELDS, AND COMPANY ACTIVITY LOCATIONS

A) Reno Hill
B) Luce Ridge, from where E and F were
   sent to the river
C) Minneconjou Ford
D) Calhoun Hill, where members from C
   and L perished
E) Where I and surviving members of C
   and L perished

F) Custer Hill, site of the "Last Stand"
G) Deep Ravine, where 28 men were slain
   on the bottom
H) Weir Point, farthest advance of the
   Reno-Benteen force

Prologue

The Sergeant Charles White Diary

Editorial note: The Sergeant Charles White diary is housed with the Walter M. Camp Papers of the Robert S. Ellison Collection, Denver Public Library, Colorado, and it is reproduced hereafter with their permission.

Sergeant Charles White (1847–1906), also known as Henry Charles Weihe, served in the Seventh Cavalry from 1871 till 1879, with a second re-enlistment from 1881 till 1886. At the time of the Custer Battle he was ranked a sergeant in M Company and was severely wounded by a gunshot wound in the right elbow during Reno's timber fight. He later rejoined the command on the bluff and was eventually evacuated on the steamer *Far West*. The account which follows was copied by Walter M. Camp in 1909 from White's private diary, loaned to him by his widow. The transcript represents the diary text of pages 17 through 24.

June 1876

At about 9 or 10 o'clock [P.M., June 24] orders were sent to the company commanders, directing them to get their companies ready at shortest notice, and that the command would march all night. At 3 o'clock [A.M., June 25] we had marched about 15 miles, and took a rest until Gen. Custer went ahead to see if he could find signs of Indians. This took him about two hours, while the General left the camp and went to the village. It is my belief that he found them sound asleep, for it was entirely too early for the Indians to be around. He returned at sunrise and the command was put in motion at once, as fast as the horses could walk.

Within five miles of the village Gen. Custer made three parties of his regiment,[1] placing Maj. Reno in command of one of these (Companies A, G, and M) and Col. Benteen in command of H, D, and K, Company B being rear guard. The men now made ready for action and everything was soon in motion at a trot or gallop for the village. First Lieutenant E. G. Mathey was in charge of the pack train.

When we arrived in sight of the first tepee [on Reno Creek] we found the Indians gone. Then a brisk trot was ordered and a detachment was sent to the front as a kind of advance guard. Lieutenant Hare[2] was in charge of this party, which consisted of Sergeants White and O'Hara, Corpl. Scollin, Blacksmith Newell, and Privates Meier, Gordon, Turley, Galenne, Braun and Thorpe.[3] These ten men moved forward until the Indians were sighted, and then Maj. Reno directed that we should join our company.

---

[1]According to the official itinerary, the division of the regiment took place shortly after crossing the divide, at 12:07 P.M., some twelve miles distant from the village.

[2]Lt. Luther R. Hare (1851–1929) of K Company was reassigned on June 24 to assist Lt. Charles A. Varnum with his duties as Chief of Scouts.

[3]Sgt. Miles F. O'Hara (1851–1876) enlisted in 1872 and served with M Company until his death on Reno's skirmish line on June 25. He had been promoted to the rank of sergeant only a few days before the battle.

Cpl. Henry M. Scollin (1851–1876), born Henry M. Cody, enlisted in 1873 and served with M Company until his death during Reno's retreat from the valley.

Blacksmith Daniel Newell (1847–1933) enlisted in 1873 and served with M Company until his discharge in 1878 upon expiration of service, and was rated a private of good character. Newell was wounded in the left thigh during the retreat up the bluffs and was later evacuated on the *Far West*.

We had now arrived at the Little Horn River and we at once proceeded to cross. By that time the column got up and orders were given to draw pistol[s] and move up in company front. Company M being [lead] company [of] the battalion, it took the right, Company G the center and Co. A the left.[4] We moved with our right resting in rear of a belt of timber, and 15 men in charge of Co. M were at once directed to deploy to the right as mounted skirmishers and to move through the timber. The first sergeant of Co. M[5] directed me to go one way and one of the drunken officers another. I am writing this not without proper proof. With my own eyes I saw these officers open a bottle of whisky and drink enough to make any ordinary man drunk. I then witnessed the greatest excitement among the intoxicated officers I ever saw.

The only officer who maintained self control and acted like an officer should do was Capt. T. H. French.[6] When the order

---

Pvt. John H. Meier (1846–1917) enlisted in 1873 and served with M Company until his discharge in 1878 upon expiration of service, and was rated a private of excellent character. Meier was wounded in the back during the Reno Hill fight and was later evacuated on the *Far West*.

Pvt. Henry Gordon (1851–1876) enlisted in 1872 and served in M Company until his death during the retreat up the bluffs.

Pvt. Henry J. Turley (1851–1876) enlisted in 1872 and served with M Company until his death during Reno's retreat from the valley.

Pvt. Jean B. D. Galenne (1849–1911) enlisted in 1873 and served in M Company until his discharge in 1878 for disability, and was rated a private of good character.

Pvt. Frank Braun (1848–1876) enlisted in 1875 and served in M Company. He was wounded in the face and left thigh during the Reno Hill fight and was later evacuated on the *Far West*. He died at Ft. Lincoln on October 4, 1876, from the trauma of his wounds.

Pvt. Rollins L. Thorpe enlisted in 1875 and served in M Company until 1876 when he was discharged for being a minor, and was rated a private of good character.

[4]The majority of evidence suggests that the mounted skirmish line advanced with M Company on the left and A Company on the right, with G Company in the rear as reserve. When the mounted advance halted, G Company took a position on the right of the skirmish line.

[5]First Sgt. John Ryan (1845–1926). He enlisted in the Seventh Cavalry in 1866 and served in M Company until his discharge in 1876 upon expiration of service, and was rated a capable and trustworthy first sergeant.

[6]Capt. Thomas H. French (1843–1882) served with the Seventh Cavalry from 1871 until his retirement in 1880. He died a pauper two years later. At the time of the Custer Battle, French commanded M Company which was assigned to Reno's battalion.

was given to dismount and fight on foot he led his company out. Lieut. Wallace[7] was then with his company and Lieut. Varnum[8] was with his company, but Col. Reno, Capt. Moylan,[9] Lieut. Hodgson[10] and Lieut. McIntosh[11] were under the shelter of the timber. The form of Capt. French could be seen towering above all the rest of the line, and I then formed my estimate of him as a brave and fearless officer, brave as a lion, and it was not whiskey that made him fearless. Two company commanders, the battalion commander and his adjutant were in the timber. Capt. Moylan was keeping himself very close.

Up to this time we had every minute been expecting reinforcements from the rear, and only two men had been wounded, but Maj. Reno appeared on the bank of the timber and ordered the men to fall [back] into the timber, mount their horses and cut their way out. In this move Maj. Reno lost his men, for the soldiers were not instructed as to the movement to be executed before starting. The men rode pell-mell through the timber and as soon as they got outside of it they were met by the Indians and shot down like buffalo.

In my own mind I have no doubt of the result of fighting

---

[7]Lt. George D. Wallace (1849–1890) served with the Seventh Cavalry from 1872 until 1890 when he was killed in action against Minneconjou Sioux at Wounded Knee. In 1876 Wallace was assigned to G Company; however, during the field campaign against the Sioux, he was reassigned to Headquarters' Staff as the Regimental Engineer.

[8]Lt. Charles A. Varnum (1849–1936) served with the Seventh Cavalry from 1872 until 1918 when he retired. In 1876 Varnum was assigned to A Company; however, during the field campaign against the Sioux, he was reassigned to Headquarters' Staff as the Chief of Scouts.

[9]Capt. Myles Moylan (1838–1909) served with the Seventh Cavalry from 1866 until 1890 when he was transferred to the Tenth Cavalry, retiring in 1893. At the time of the Custer Battle, Moylan commanded A Company which was assigned to Reno's battalion.

[10]Lt. Benjamin H. Hodgson (1848–1876) served with the Seventh Cavalry from 1870 until his death during Reno's retreat from the valley. In 1876 Hodgson was assigned to B Company; however, during the field campaign against the Sioux, he was reassigned to Reno's staff as the Acting Adjutant of the battalion.

[11]Lt. Donald McIntosh (1838–1876) served in the Seventh Cavalry from 1867 until his death during Reno's retreat from the valley. At the time of the Custer Battle, McIntosh commanded G Company which was assigned to Reno's battalion.

Indians from the timber as shelter, and they all tell me that timber is the best shelter that white troops can get into when they were outnumbered by Indians. It is my firm belief that had Maj. Reno held the timber in which his men were formed, and near the village, those Indians who attacked us first would certainly have been compelled to remain there, instead of going to the assistance of Crazy Horse, who was ordered by Sitting Bull to cut Custer off, which he did, and with the combined forces accomplished Custer's defeat. Had Reno held the timber we could have moved into the village and set it on fire very quickly in event of their leaving our front, as they did do when we retreated across the river. (He makes no mention here of being left in the timber when Reno retreated out of it—[W. M. Camp.])[12]

When I got back to the command I went to the hospital and received medical treatment for my wound, and went to bed. Our position had then been selected by Col. Benteen. He was the only officer present whom we could rely upon, and he behaved well. During the engagement on the hill on the 26th he was constantly where the bullets were the thickest, encouraging the men. Lieut. E. G. Mathey[13] went to the hospital during the firing in the afternoon of the 25th and [remained there] up to 10 A.M. on the 26th, when he got ashamed of himself and took a carbine and joined Capt. Moylan, who lay behind some dead mules that had been shot during the engagement.[14] The most cowardly officers I ever

---

[12]Abandoned in the timber, Sgt. White and twelve other soldiers were guided across the river by a civilian scout named George Herendeen, and arrived safely on Reno Hill nearly two hours after Reno's retreat had started.

[13]Lt. Edward G. Mathey (1837–1915) served with the Seventh Cavalry from 1867 until 1896 when he retired due to disability. In 1876 Mathey was assigned to M Company; however, during the field campaign against the Sioux, he was reassigned to command the pack train.

[14]Rumors of Lt. Edward Mathey's timid behavior during the Reno Hill fight did not escape Capt. Benteen who later wrote that Mathey had shown the white feather. Capt. Myles Moylan's behavior was similarly scorned by the enlisted men who noticed that he had lain behind a pack saddle during most of the Reno Hill fight. He was given the derisive nickname of "Aparejo Mickie."

saw were there and [also] some of the bravest whom I have ever seen.

The men lost from my company in retreating out of the bottom were Sergeant O'Hara, Corpl. Scollin, Corpl. Stringer, Privates Gordon, Klotzbucher, Lorentz, Smith, Summers, and Turley.[15] (He has omitted Meyer[16]—[W. M.

[15]Sgt. Miles F. O'Hara was the first soldier wounded on the skirmish line and pleaded with his comrades not to abandon him in his disabled condition; his pleas were ignored. After the battle Sgt. John Ryan searched for O'Hara, but could not locate the remains and assumed that the Indians had thrown the body in the river. However, a skull and mandible found among rotted remnants of yellow-striped trousers, discovered on Reno's skirmish line by Surgeon Robert Shufeldt in 1877, may well have been the mortal remains of Sgt. O'Hara.

Cpl. Henry M. Scollin was unhorsed during the retreat and was rescued by Pvt. Rollins L. Thorpe with whom he rode double. However, Thorpe's horse lost its footing while crossing a boggy hollow near the river, where Scollin was killed. His body was extremely mutilated, with the right leg severed from the trunk. The remains were buried by Sgt. John Ryan who accomplished the identification through the corporal stripes on the victim's trousers.

Born Frederick Stressinger (1852–1876), Cpl. Frederick Streing, aka Frederick Stringer, enlisted in 1872 and served in M Company until his death on June 25 when he was mortally wounded on the skirmish line in the timber, and stood leaning against a tree when last seen alive by his comrades.

Pvt. Henry Gordon was killed on June 25 by a bullet in the neck while ascending the bluffs on the east side of the river. His remains were extremely mutilated.

Pvt. Henry Klotzbucher (1848–1876) enlisted in 1873 and served in M Company until his death in the timber on June 25 when he was mortally wounded by a gunshot to the abdomen. His unmolested remains were identified after the battle.

Pvt. George Lorentz (1851–1876) enlisted in 1872 and served with M Company until his death in the timber on June 25 when he was killed by a gunshot to the back of the head. Lorentz had been assigned to Capt. French as his orderly.

Pvt. George E. Smith (1850–1876) enlisted in 1875 and served in M Company until his death on June 25 when his unruly horse bolted from the skirmish line straight into the Indian village. His remains were not recovered.

Pvt. David "Sandy" Summers (1848–1876) enlisted in May of 1876 and served with M Company until June 25 when he was killed just outside the timber as he emerged from the woods at the start of the retreat. His remains were extremely mutilated.

Pvt. Henry J. Turley was killed by a volley during the retreat and was found on the east side of the river, some twenty feet from the body of Lt. Hodgson. Turley's body was disfigured by his own hunting knife, which had been driven to the hilt into his right eye socket.

[16]Pvt. William D. "Tinker Bill" Meyer (1853–1876) enlisted in 1875 and served with M Company as its company farrier until his death on June 25 when a bullet crashed into his left temple during the ascent of the bluffs. The impact of the projectile splattered blood onto the face of Pvt. Edward Pigford who was near the victim and witnessed his death.

Camp.]) Privates Tanner and Voight were killed on the hill.[17] The ten men killed in the valley were only wounded when they fell from their horses and were finished up by about fifty Indian arrows when the Indians were making for Custer's column.

Sergeant Thomas McLaughlin,[18] of Co. H, told Maj. Reno that there should be some one sent to rescue the wounded, and Reno remarked that the Sergeant might get a detail and rescue them himself, if he wanted to. The poor wounded were butchered in sight of the seven companies, and there was no officer brave enough to go to help them. This had a discouraging effect on the men. If Col. Benteen had been in command there would have been a different tale to tell.

On the morning of the 27th Gen. [John] Gibbon's column came in sight, as agreed to by General Terry. Custer and Gibbon were expected to communicate with each other by couriers, but Gen. Custer, being insane (he probably means to say rash, White being a German and not well acquainted with the language—[W. M. Camp]), we did not expect anything better from him than disobedience of orders which he received from his superior officer.

---

[17]Pvt. James J. Tanner (1849–1876), born Jacob Henry Gebhart, enlisted in 1875 and served in M Company until his death on June 26 when he was mortally wounded during Capt. Benteen's charge on the Indians at the south side of Reno Hill. Tanner was carried back to the trenches by Sgt. John Ryan and died in the field hospital during the early afternoon. His remains were buried on Reno Hill on the evening of June 26. In 1903 his fragile bones were exhumed and transferred to the National Cemetery near Custer Hill. Tanner had been a water carrier.

Pvt. Henry C. Voight (1855–1876) enlisted in 1873 and served with M Company until his death on June 25 when he was killed instantly on Reno Hill by a gunshot to the head. Voight died while untangling the dead horse of Capt. French from a set of frightened horses. When the fury of battle subsided that evening, Voight was found lying stretched out in death while still holding the reins of the four horses. He was buried alongside James Tanner on Reno Hill on the evening of June 26. In 1903 his fragile remains were exhumed and transferred to the National Cemetery near Custer Hill.

[18]Sgt. Thomas F. McLaughlin (1847–1886) served in the Seventh Cavalry from 1868 until 1876 when he was discharged upon expiration of service, and was rated a sergeant of excellent character. At the time of the Custer Battle, he was assigned to H Company. McLaughlin was wounded in the left arm during the defense of Reno Hill, but returned to active duty after treatment in the field hospital.

On the 29th we were landed safely at the boat, where we took as comfortable places as we could find. The officers of the other regiments were very kind to us, but our own officers kept their distance, with the exception of Col. Weir[19]—he was very kind and considerate toward the wounded, and they all remembered him for that.

After getting to the mouth of the Big Horn we were moved from the boat, and, on July 2, what was left of the expedition was moved over to the left bank of the Yellowstone. On the 3rd day of July all the wounded were put on board the steamer and at 11 A.M. the Far West proceeded downstream. On the boat three of the wounded men died.[20] We arrived at Bismarck on the evening of July 6th, but too late to cross over to Ft. A. Lincoln, so we waited until the next morning. The boat was draped in mourning and the flag was at half mast as we pulled into the landing, which told those standing on shore that something terrible had happened. There were 29 widows who heard the sad news that day. The weeping, wailing and pulling of hair which followed the spreading of the unwelcome information caused even men to tremble.

---

[19]Capt. Thomas B. Weir (1838–1876) served with the Seventh Cavalry from 1866 until his sudden death in 1876 while on recruiting services in New York. During the Custer Battle, Capt. Weir commanded D Company which was assigned to Benteen's battalion.

[20]The names of these three casualties are as follows.

Cpl. George H. King (1848–1876) of A Company. He was wounded in the left shoulder on the evening of June 25 and was evacuated on the Far West. He died aboard the steamer on July 2 from complications of his wound and was buried on the north bank of the Yellowstone near the mouth of the Big Horn River. His remains were later transferred to the National Cemetery near Custer Hill, Grave B-8.

Pvt. William M. George (1846–1876) of H Company. He was wounded in the left side on Reno Hill and was evacuated on the Far West. He suffered greatly from the complications of his wound and died aboard the steamer at 4 A.M. on July 3. His remains were buried on the river bank near the mouth of the Powder River.

Pvt. James C. Bennett (1848–1876) of C Company. He was paralyzed by a gunshot to the spine on June 26 while reinforcing H Company's line. He was evacuated on the Far West and died aboard the steamer at 3 P.M. on July 5 near Ft. Lincoln.

The Dry Hide, Red Cloud, and Howling Eagle Statement

Editorial note: The Dry Hide, Red Cloud, and Howling Eagle statements are contained in a report by John D. Miles, U.S. Indian Agent at the Cheyenne and Arapahoe Agency, Darlington, Indian Territory. This document was filed with the Office of the Adjutant General, Consolidated File 3770 AGO, Records of the War Department, National Archives, Washington, D.C. A subject search failed to disclose any data on the three Cheyenne informants.

Darlington, Indian Territory
August 4, 1876

I [John D. Miles] have the honor to report the arrival at this Agency on the 29th ult from the Red Cloud Agency three Cheyenne young men, Dry Hide, Red Cloud, [and] Howling Eagle. They were first required to report to Col. Mizner, commanding Fort Reno, where they were disarmed and dismounted and afterwards turned over to me with [the] Sand Hill[1] and White Antelope[2] parties.

---

[1]Sand Hill was a Southern Cheyenne chief of the Aorta Band who was married to a Sioux woman. He was involved in the capture of Mary (continued on next page)

They report having been on the way only fourteen (14) days [from the Red Cloud Agency]. They say they ran onto a large party of Indians believed to be Utes, on the headwaters of the Republican, who gave them a close chase, capturing all their ponies but one, and very nearly captured their party. Afterwards they were obliged to walk most of the time as only one could ride, and it was with some difficulty that they could obtain necessary food. Their necessities soon gave way and they were left barefoot.

They report that Dull Knife[3] and Hawk,[4] Northern Cheyennes, are still at the Agency, and talk of coming south; [they] say that numerous messengers have arrived from the

---

Fletcher on the North Platte in 1865 and later released her unharmed to his Indian agent, Maj. Edward W. Wynkoop. In the spring of 1875 Sand Hill left his southern agency with his wife, his son Yellow Horse, and a small following with intentions to join the Northern Cheyennes. While camped along Sappa Creek, Kansas, on April 23 they were attacked by a detachment of the Sixth cavalry, resulting in the death of nineteen Cheyennes. Although Sand Hill was severely wounded during the fight, he and his family managed to escape and eventually reached the Northern Cheyennes.

[2]White Antelope was a Southern Cheyenne chief of the Dog Soldier Band who was regarded among his people as one of the bravest leaders. In 1874 he and a small following of thirteen lodges left their southern agency and joined the Northern Cheyennes at Red Cloud Agency, Nebraska. He participated in the Camp Robinson Outbreak of January 10, 1879, and committed suicide by stabbing himself to death after his infant child was killed and his wife was mortally wounded by soldiers.

[3]Dull Knife was one of the four principal chiefs of the Northern Cheyennes. In his younger years he had been a war chief, and although known as a brave and skilled fighter, it was said that he neither organized nor planned his battles. In 1876 Dull Knife's village was destroyed by Gen. Ranald S. MacKenzie, which resulted in the surrender of his band in 1877 and their subsequent removal to Indian Territory. However, due to deplorable health conditions in the south, Dull Knife led his band on an epic trek to their northern homeland in 1878 and eventually surrendered at Red Cloud Agency. They steadfastly refused to go back to their southern agency and were imprisoned at Camp Robinson where they were subjected to starvation, leading to their disastrous attempt to escape on January 10, 1879. Of the 150 people in his band, some seventy men, women, and children were indiscriminately killed as a result of the actions of an incompetent post commander and the inhumanity of the War Department. Dull Knife died in 1883, a broken-hearted old man who was haunted by memories of the slaughter of his people, including his own son and daughter.

[4]Hawk was a Southern Cheyenne leader of the Dog Soldier Band who joined the Northern Cheyennes after the decimation of his people at Summit Springs, July 11, 1869, by troops of the Fifth Cavalry and Pawnee Indian Scouts.

hostile camps at the Red Cloud Agency, and report that in the Crook fight some time ago [June 17, 1876], 8 Sioux and 3 Cheyennes were killed, among the latter was Little Shield[5] formerly of this Agency and one of the O. F. Short and Germain [sic] massacre.[6] Yellow Horse,[7] son of Sand Hill, was in the engagement, but escaped unharmed. Messengers arriving from the Custer fight, brought in with them to the Agency, sugar, coffee, arms, horses and some scalps, around which dances were kept up.

I enclose herewith a diagram which will give you some idea of the Custer fight from an Indian standpoint, as related by these Indians who heard messengers relate the fight. The red line will indicate Custer's approach to the camps of about 50 lodges, on the Rosebud who, being appraised of his approach, made a hasty march to the Little Big Horn, going into camp at the extreme north end of the main Sioux and Cheyenne camp.

Custer, crossing the Rosebud, discovered the deserted camp and took [t]his trail as indicated by the red line, attacking [with Reno's battalion] the last mentioned camp just

---

[5]Little Shield was not a battle casualty of the Rosebud Fight. The majority of Cheyenne sources indicate that only one Cheyenne was killed and that his name was Black Sun, nicknamed Scabby, who was known to the Sioux as Alligator. Little Shield was a Southern Cheyenne and a chief of the Elk Scrapers Society. He participated in the Custer Fight, and after the surrender of the Cheyennes in 1877 he was relocated in Indian Territory. Little Shield left his southern agency in 1878 and surrendered with Dull Knife at Red Cloud Agency, Nebraska. He was imprisoned at Camp Robinson and led the disastrous outbreak of January 10, 1879, killing one of the military guards.

[6]Surveyor Oliver F. Short and five members of his survey crew were slain on August 26, 1874, near Ft. Dodge, Kansas, by a Cheyenne war party of Bowstring warriors under Medicine Water. This same war party was also responsible for the attack on John German and his immigrant family on September 11, 1874, on the Smoky Hill road near the present Kansas-Colorado border. John German and his wife Lydia, their son Stephen, and their older daughters Rebecca and Joanna were all killed, while four younger daughters, Adalaide, Catherina, Julia, and Sophia were taken captive. Adalaide and Julia were rescued by troops on November 8, 1874, while the two older sisters were released by the Cheyennes upon their surrender in March of 1875.

[7]Yellow Horse was the son of Sand Hill, a Southern Cheyenne, and was a survivor of the Sappa Creek Fight.

before daylight, killing some men, women, and children, the camp stampeding or retreating in the direction of the main camp, and just at daylight Custer [himself] came down on the camp with a charge; but in the meantime his attack had been sounded throughout the entire camp [and] preparation had been made for his reception.[8]

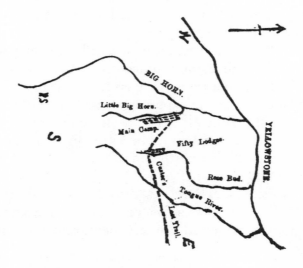

As will be seen by the *red line* [reproduced in black on the map], Custer [detached Reno who] led the charge from the camps of 50 lodges in the direction of the main village, but was met with such a terrific fire from the Indians who had by this time gained superior advantage from the hills, as to force him into and across a big "slough, or bayou" (a point well known to all the Northern Indians), in which many of his horses mired, and sixty (60) of his men were killed in this

---

[8]At daylight, June 25, Custer's troops were still in bivouac on the east slope of the Wolf Mountain divide. This divide separates the Rosebud from the Little Bighorn which runs on the west side. Reno's attack on the Indian camp did not take place until about 3 o'clock in the afternoon.

"slough" and afterwards dragged out by the Indians, and stripped of all valuables and generally scalped.[9]

Custer [Reno] then with the balance of his troops endeavored to cross the river and make his way out through the hills on the opposite side of the river, but was unable to do so from the fact of the steepness of the bank. Failing in this move and, as the Indians believe, fully realizing the trap into which he had been drawn, he recrossed [a bend in] the river, thinking that he might possibly cut his way back through the Indian camp, and escape by the way he came in, but the Indians claim to have had 40 warriors to every *one* of Custer's men, and once demoralized [they] were an easy prey to the enraged Sioux and Cheyennes, only waiting to exterminate the whole party.

After the return from the attempt to cross the river, the struggle was a hand to hand fight, Custer leading his band to the right, and then back down the river to the point where they were first forced into the "slough", where they were so completely surrounded as to be unable to escape in any direction, and most of those remaining living were dragged from their horses and killed.

Custer and a few others did succeed in riding through and over his enemy, and reached an eminence near by, only to be met by *thousands* on the surrounding hill, where he met the same fate as his whole command.

The Indians say that after the troops were driven into the "slough" they were completely demoralized, and were an easy

---

[9]Since the Indians did not know who Reno was—in fact, did not know that he commanded a separate battalion—the movements of Reno's troops were referred to by the Indians as Custer's movements, which causes confusion in our perception of their accounts. Besides being difficult to comprehend, the narrative and the map are incorrect as to the location of the Indian village, which was erected on the west side of the river and *not* on the east bank. It should be kept in mind, however, that the three young informants were not present at the battle, and that their statements were based on hearsay information obtained at Red Cloud Agency from warriors who partook in the fight. This fact may have added to the contradictions in their recounting.

prey, showing or giving but little resistance. Each one seemed trying to escape instead of trying to fight. They report that Crazy Horse[10] and Sitting Bull[11] were not killed, and that less than sixty (60) Sioux and Cheyennes were killed, the greater portion being killed during the first fire before daybreak. The whole engagement did not last over one hour from the time of the first "charge".

---

[10]Crazy Horse (1840–1877) was an Oglala Lakota and the war leader of the hostile Northern Sioux. He was elected to the Office of Shirt Wearer in 1868 and served the Oglala people till 1870 when he was forced to resign. He was a member of the Strongheart Society and the Last Child Lodge. Crazy Horse surrendered in May of 1877 and was bayonetted to death on September 5, 1877, at Camp Robinson, Nebraska.

[11]Sitting Bull (1831–1890) was a Hunkpapa Lakota shaman and the spiritual leader of the hostile Northern Sioux. He was a member of the Silent Eaters and the Strong Heart Society. Known for his contempt for the whites, he was killed by the Standing Rock Indian Police while resisting arrest on December 15, 1890.

The Little Buck Elk Statement

Editorial note: The Little Buck Elk statement is contained in a report by Thomas J. Mitchell, U.S. Indian Agent at the Milk River Indian Agency, Fort Peck, Montana Territory. This document was filed with the Office of the Adjutant General, Consolidated File 3770 AGO, Records of the War Department, National Archives, Washington, D.C. A subject search failed to disclose any data on this Hunkpapa eyewitness.

Fort Peck, Montana Territory
September 23, 1876

[Little Buck Elk says] that the Uncpapa camp is about twenty miles south of the mouth of the Powder River, on Beaver Creek; that another large camp is about the same distance south of the Uncpapas, near Blue Earth Hills, and the Arapahoes and Cheyennes are camped at the forks of Tongue River in the Red Hills, twenty or twenty-five miles distant from the last camp.

Sitting Bull sent him to ascertain whether I [Indian Agent Thomas J. Mitchell] would allow the hostiles to come in and trade for ammunition. I dispatched a messenger to his camp, informing him that they could get no ammunition here, or on this reservation, but if they desire to come in, surrender their arms and all government property in their possession, I would treat them kindly and provide for them until I could receive instructions from you. I will receive a reply from Sitting Bull within ten days or two weeks.

Little Buck Elk stated that he was in the fight in which Gen. Custer and all of his men were slaughtered; and that eleven different tribes were engaged in the fight.[1] He states that "the Indians were as thick as bees at the fight;" that there were so many of them, they could not all take part in it; that some men call the soldiers cowards, but they were not, [and that instead] they were all brave men and fought well; that some of them when they found themselves surrounded and overpowered, broke through the lines and tried to make their escape, but were pursued and killed miles from the battle-ground.[2] One soldier who had a faster horse than the rest, made his escape into the badlands, and after he had ridden seven or eight miles from where the fight took place, accidently ran into a war party of Indians, and was killed by them. This soldier rode a big horse with flaxen mane and had a gov-

---

[1]The Indian people attacked at the Little Bighorn belonged to the Sioux, the Cheyenne, and the Arapaho nations. The Sioux tribes present are dialectically identified as a) Lakota speakers: the Hunkpapa, the Blackfoot, the Two Kettle, the Sans Arc, the Minneconjou, the Brule, and the Oglala; b) Nakota speakers: the Yankton and the Yanktonai; and c) Dakota speakers: the Santee.

[2]As early as 1877 rumors began to circulate that a detachment of some twenty soldiers had been killed at a considerable distance from the battlefield. The original source of this information was a Crow Scout named Curley who related that Cheyennes had told him of the killing of some thirty soldiers near the top of the Wolf Mountain divide. A *Chicago Tribune* despatch in August of 1877 confirmed Curley's statement and reported that Crow Indians had found the skeletons of about twenty-five soldiers, some fifteen miles from the battlefield. In an attempt to verify these rumors, Lt. Charles F. Roe and a troop of Second Cavalry was dispatched to the battlefield in 1881. They combed the area as far as the Wolf Mountains, but failed to find any trace of these alleged missing men. Roe's findings are supported by the personnel reduction on the muster rolls of 1876, taken before and after the battle. Since the sum difference on these rolls is nearly identical to the official burial count, it confirms that all the bodies had indeed been accounted for.

ernment saddle with grey saddle blanket; but it was not known whether he was an officer or not.

He states that they captured six battle flags,[3] and that no soldiers were taken alive, but after the fight the women went among the dead bodies and robbed and mutilated them. That after Custer and his men were "wiped out," they attacked Reno and surrounded his command on a hill; that the soldiers dug holes and got into them, and fought the Indians, but if Gen. Terry's forces had not come up when they did, Reno with his entire force would have been "wiped out" also.

He states further that there were plenty of watches and money taken from the bodies of the dead soldiers, and that the young men are now wearing them in their shirts and belts. He promised me that if the watch belonging to Lieut. Crittenden could be found he would deliver it to me.[4]

He says they have tried to keep the number [of casualties]

---

[3]Of the five company guidons lost by Custer's battalion, one was recovered by Sgt. Ferdinand Culbertson who found the blood-stained cloth on Custer's battlefield hidden under the remains of a soldier. Unfortunately, we do not know to which company this guidon belonged because the application of letters on the swallow-tailed flags had been discontinued in 1862. We also know that Custer's headquarters flag was lost, allegedly captured by an Oglala named Stand First. The regimental flag, however was not lost because it was stored with the headquarters' baggage carried with the pack train.

Of the three flags carried with Reno's battalion, we know that A Company's guidon was left in the timber where Sgt. Henry Fehler abandoned it at the start of the retreat. Although Lt. DeRudio made an attempt to recover the guidon, the infiltration of Indians into the woods prevented DeRudio from doing so. M Company's guidon was taken to Reno Hill by Cpl. Frank Sniffin who had torn the flag from its staff and carried it safely inside his blouse. We do not know the whereabouts of G Company's guidon. However, according to the Oglala, Red Feather, one of Reno's flags was captured on the skirmish line in the valley, which, by exclusion, could only be the guidon carried by G Company.

[4]Lt. John J. Crittenden served with the 20th Infantry from 1875 until May 1876 when he requested a combat assignment with the Seventh Cavalry, despite the recent loss of his left eye. After the battle, Crittenden's mutilated body was found on Calhoun Hill, bristling with arrows. One of the arrows had been shot in his left eye socket and had fragmented his glass eye. His remains were initially buried on Calhoun Hill, but were exhumed in 1931 and reinterred in the cemetery near Custer Hill, Grave A-601. Crittenden's watch was recovered in Canada from one of Sitting Bull's warriors and was returned to Crittenden's father after the ownership was established in England through a Liverpool watchmaker.

lost by them from being known, but that it is no use of lying about it, for the truth will come out some time that they have over one hundred Indians killed in the fight;[5] but it was not known at the time of the fight that Gen. Custer was in command and was killed.

I [Thomas J. Mitchell] told him that I had understood that Lieut. Crittenden was the only child of his parents, and that his death had almost broken their hearts. His answer was, "*Me Sunko*, you say that the parents of Lieut. Crittenden loved him; that he was their only child; and that they were sorely grieved at his death: You can judge of the grief and anguish of the parents of the nine young men found by the whites after the battle, lying dead in the [funeral] lodge. They were all brave and good, yes, fine young men and the grief of the parents is great."

He states that after Gen. Terry and Crook formed a junction, the army marched within full view of the Indian camps, but the soldiers did not offer to attack them, nor they the soldiers. He states the hostiles do not want to fight the soldiers, but they have joined together to drive the whites out of the Black Hills; that whites had sent presents of tobacco to the hostile camps, and wanted them to go to the lower Agencies to make a treaty of peace, but Sitting Bull objected to their going-in yet. . . .

In reply to the question, where did you get your ammunition? he answered, ["]The soldiers brought it to us (meaning that they had taken it from the bodies of the dead soldiers), and the traders from the Burning Ground furnished us with some.["] He states that the Burning Ground embraces a country extending from south of the Black Hills to the Platte River. . . .

---

[5]Comparison of reliable casualty counts reveals that the Indians sustained a loss of about forty people, of which seven were Cheyennes and thirty-three were Sioux, including ten women and children. Thirty-seven individuals died during the combat on June 25 and 26, while three others later succumbed to the trauma of their wounds.

The Crazy Horse Interview

Editorial note: The Crazy Horse interview is contained in a special telegram from Camp Robinson, which was printed in the *Chicago Times* issue of May 26, 1877.

Crazy Horse (1840–1877) was the son of the Oglala known as Worm and the Minneconjou woman Rattle Blanket. As a result of his remarkable ability to distinguish himself in combat, Crazy Horse was elected in 1868 to the office of Scalp Shirt Wearer, civil leaders who were entrusted with the government of the Oglala tribe. In 1871 Crazy Horse married the Oglala woman Black Shawl who bore him his only child, a daughter named Afraid of Her, who died in 1873 from frail health. After the Sioux Wars, Crazy Horse and his band surrendered at Fort Robinson, Nebraska, where he was stabbed to death by a soldier while resisting arrest on September 5, 1877.

Horned Horse was an Oglala band leader and a close ally of Crazy Horse. A second account attributed to Horned Horse is printed hereafter. Red Dog was the prominent leader of the *Ohyuhpe* Band, one of the strongest and oldest groups among the Northern Oglalas. The account which follows was obtained by Charles Diehl while on special assignment for the *Chicago Times*.

Camp Robinson, Nebraska
May 24, 1877

Your correspondent has obtained some very valuable information in regard to the Custer massacre from Crazy Horse through Horned Horse as his spokesman, which is authentic and confirmed by other principal chiefs. I interviewed these chiefs this afternoon, Lieut. Clark[1] arranging the meeting and Wm. Hunter[2] acting as interpreter, a man perfectly reliable and thoroughly conversant with the Indian language. This is the Indian version, and the first published.

The attack was made on the village by a strong force at 11 o'clock in the morning at the upper end of the village. This was the force commanded by Maj. Reno, and very shortly afterward the lower end of the village was attacked by another strong force, that commanded by Custer.

The village was divided into seven different bands of Indians, each commanded by a separate chief, and extended in nearly a straight line. The bands were in the order mentioned

---

[1]Lt. William P. Clark, Second Cavalry, was assigned as military Indian agent at Ft. Robinson, Nebraska in December 1876 and placed in charge of the U.S. Indian Scouts. He was a confidant to Gen. George Crook, commander of the Department of the Platte, with whom he was in constant communication regarding the volatile state of affairs at Red Cloud Agency. After the ill-fated removal of the Lakotas to the Missouri River late in 1877, Clark was relieved from his special assignment and returned to duty with Company K, Second Cavalry. Known to the Indians as White Hat, Clark was an expert in sign communication and was directed by Gen. William T. Sherman in 1881 to compile a manual for use by army officers. Clark had barely finished his research in 1884 when he suddenly died. His work was published in 1885 under the title *The Indian Sign Language.*

[2]William Hunter (1855–1929), better known as William "Billy" Garnett, was born near Ft. Laramie as the son of Gen. Richard B. Garnett and an Oglala woman named Looks at Him. After Gen. Garnett's death at Gettysburg in 1863, his wife eventually married John Hunter, and although the latter was slain in a gunfight near Ft. Laramie in 1868, it was Hunter's last name by which William was known to the Army in 1877. Eventually Billy discarded the Hunter name and became known only by the last name of his natural father. Although he later reconciled with the wealthy Garnett family, Billy continued to live with his mother's Oglala people and died at Pine Ridge in 1929. From 1876 till 1878, William Garnett was employed by the Army at Ft. Robinson as a guide, interpreter and chief of Indian scouts.

below, commencing from the lower end, where Custer made his attack: First, the Uncapapas, under Sitting Bull; second, the Oglalas, under Crazy Horse; third, the Minneconjous, under Fast Bull; fourth, the Sans Arcs, under Red Bear; fifth, the Cheyennes, under Ice Bear,[3] their two principal chiefs being absent; sixth, the Santees and Yanktonais, under Red Point,[4] of the Santees; seventh, the Blackfeet, under Scabby Head.[5]

The village consisted of eighteen hundred lodges, and at least four hundred wickiups, a lodge made of small poles and willows for temporary shelter. Each of the wickiups contained four young bucks, and the estimate made by Crazy Horse is that each lodge had from three to four warriors. Estimating at three made a fighting force of over seven thousand Indians. This is the lowest estimate that can be made, for there were a good many Indians without shelters, hangers-on, who fought when called upon, and the usual number was much above seven thousand.

The attack was a surprise and totally unlooked for. When Custer made his charge the women, papooses, children, in

---

[3]Ice Bear, also known as White Bear or Polar Bear, was the Lakota name for the Cheyenne White Bull (1834–1910), who was a respected shaman among the Northern Cheyennes. His son, Noisy Walking, was mortally wounded on Custer's battlefield on June 25.

[4]Red Point, or *Inkpa Duta* 'Bloody Antler Point,' also known as Red Top, was the patriarch leader of a Santee band which found sanctuary in Canada after the Sioux uprising in Minnesota in 1862. In the fall of 1875, Red Point and some twenty lodges of his Santee band came south from Manitoba and joined Sitting Bull's Northern Hunkpapas. One of the Santees with Red Top was White Foot Print, the uncle of Dr. Charles Eastman, agency physician at Pine Ridge.

[5]Contemporary sources suggest that the lodges of the Blackfeet, the Hunkpapas, along with some Santee, Yanktonai, and a few Two Kettles, were all grouped together in a large circle at the south end of the great village where Reno made his attack. Further north, on the bench land along the river, was the tribal circle of the Sans Arcs, followed by the lodges of the Minneconjous, who camped across from the mouth of Medicine Tail Ford, also known as Minneconjou Ford. West of the Minneconjou circle, away from the river, stood the lodges of the Oglalas and some Brules, while north of them were the Cheyennes, who camped near the river and not far from the Minneconjou circle.

fact all that were not fighters made a stampede in a northerly direction. Custer, seeing so numerous a body, mistook them for the main body of Indians retreating and abandoning their village, and immediately gave pursuit. The warriors in the village, seeing this, divided their forces into two parts, one intercepting Custer between their non-combatants and him, and the other getting in his rear. Outnumbering him as they did, they had him at their mercy, and the dreadful massacre ensued.

Horned Horse says the smoke and dust was so great that foe could not be distinguished from friend. The horses were wild with fright and uncontrollable. The Indians were knocking each other from their steeds, and it is an absolute fact that the young bucks in their excitement and fury killed each other, several dead Indians being found killed by arrows.[6] Horned Horse represented this hell of fire and smoke and death by intertwining his fingers and saying: "Just like this, Indians and white men." Three chiefs say they suffered a loss of fifty-eight killed, and over sixty wounded. From their way of expressing it, I should judge about 60 per cent of their wounded died.

While this butchery was going on, Reno was fighting in the upper part of the village, but did not get in so as to get surrounded, and managed to escape. They say had he got in as far, he would have suffered the same fate as Custer; but he retreated to the bluffs, and was held there until the Indians fighting Custer, comprising over half the village, could join the northern portion in besieging him. These Indians claim that but for the timely arrival of Gen. Terry, they would have

---

[6]During the fight on Custer's battlefield, several Indians were killed after being mistaken for Ree or Crow army scouts seen earlier with Reno's battalion. One such incident took place on Calhoun Hill where an Arapaho named Left Hand lanced a Hunkpapa to death, mistaking him for an enemy. A similar incident occurred in Deep Ravine where a hasty Sioux shot a Cheyenne boy named Noisy Walking, while others lanced him through the chest.

certainly got Reno. They would have surrounded and stormed him out, or would have besieged and eventually captured him. From what I know of Crazy Horse, I should say that he no doubt is capable of conducting a siege. In both the Rosebud fight and the Custer massacre the Indians claim he rode unarmed in the thickness of the fight, invoking the blessing of the Great Spirit on him—that if he was right he might be victorious, and if wrong that he might be killed.[7]

. . . No one was present at the interview with your correspondent but the chiefs and [the] interpreter. Hesitation was at first manifested, but after some questioning and talking on minor topics, Horned Horse told his story readily, which met with the approval of Crazy Horse and Red Dog,[8] a friendly agency Indian, who were present.

---

[7]Crazy Horse arrived late at the Reno fight because of his lengthy incantations to invoke the spiritual powers for both himself and his pony. These rites took so much time that the young men of his soldier's lodge could hardly restrain their impatience with the delay. Nonetheless, Crazy Horse was instrumental in the destruction of Keogh's company by breaking the soldiers' line in two after making several mounted charges. He was reverently called "Our Brave Man" by members of his tribe, while other Lakotas remembered his charisma during the fight, stating that everyone became brave when Crazy Horse appeared on the battlefield.

[8]Red Dog, leader of the *Ohyuhpe* Oglala band, was married to a sister of Red Cloud and maintained close ties with the Bad Face Band. Contemporary sources describe Red Dog as an orator, with a heavy build and an intelligent face. His family was the keeper of the band's Winter Count, which was later kept by Red Dog's son, Cloud Shield.

The Horned Horse Statement

Editorial note: The Horned Horse statement is contained in John F. Finerty, *War-path and Bivouac: The Bighorn and Yellowstone Expedition* (The Lakeside Press: Chicago, IL, 1955), pp. 208–211.

Horned Horse was an Oglala band leader whose son, White Eagle, was killed during the Reno battle. His second son, White Cow Walking, survived the battle and told his experiences to Walter Campbell in an interview which is printed herein. The account which follows was obtained by John F. Finerty, a Chicago newspaper reporter, during an interview with Lt. William P. Clark about 1877. Clark was then the acting military Indian agent for the Oglalas at Camp Robinson, Nebraska. The map appended to this statement was copied by Clark from a rude map drawn on a dirt floor during an interview with an unidentified Oglala. The map maker may well have been Horned Horse.

[Camp Robinson, 1877]

Horned Horse, an old Sioux chief, whose son was killed early in the fight,[1] stated to the late Capt. [William] Philo

---

[1] The name of this son was White Eagle. He was killed on the west slope of Reno Hill while pursuing soldiers on their ascent up the bluffs. He was the only Oglala slain during the valley fight.

Clark, after the surrender of the hostiles,[2] that he went up on a hill overlooking the field to mourn for the dead, as he was too weak to fight, after the Indian fashion. He had a full view of all that took place almost from the beginning.

The Little Big Horn is a stream filled with dangerous quicksand, and cuts off the edges of the northern bluffs sharply near the point where Custer perished. The Indians first saw the troops on the bluffs early in the morning, but, owing to the abruptness and height of the river banks, Custer could not get down to the edge of the stream.

The valley of the Little Big Horn is from half a mile to a mile and a half wide, and along it for a distance of fully five miles the mighty Indian village stretched. Most of the immense pony herd was out grazing when the savages took the alarm at the appearance of the troops on the heights. The warriors ran at once for their arms, but by the time they had taken up their guns and ammunition belts, the soldiers had disappeared.[3] The Indians thought they had been frightened off by the evident strength of the village, but again, after what seemed quite a long interval, the head of Custer's column showed itself coming down a dry watercourse, which formed a narrow ravine, toward the river's edge.[4] He made a dash to get across, but was met by such a tremendous fire from the repeating rifles of the savages that the head of his command reeled back toward the bluffs after losing several men who tumbled into the water, which was there but eighteen inches

---

[2]Horned Horse surrendered with Crazy Horse's band at Camp Robinson on May 12, 1877. The census taken at the surrender reveals that the Horned Horse lodge was occupied by seven people: Horned Horse, Sees the Cow, At the End, three females, and one male child.

[3]This statement has reference to Custer's battalion. The narrative ignores Reno's approach and subsequent attack.

[4]The description of Custer's route matches present Medicine Tail Coulee and its drainage. Across from Medicine Tail Ford, on the west bank, the Minneconjous had erected their lodges. Horned Horse's band of Oglalas camped near the Minneconjous, but farther back from the river.

deep, and were swallowed up in the quicksand. This is considered an explanation of the disappearance of Lieutenant Harrington and several men whose bodies were not found on the field of battle. They were not made prisoners by the Indians, nor did any of them succeed in breaking through the thick array of infuriated savages.

Horned Horse did not recognize Custer, but supposed he was the officer who led the column that attempted to cross the stream. Custer then sought to lead his men up to the bluffs by a diagonal movement, all of them having dismounted, and firing, whenever they could, over the backs of their horses at the Indians, who by that time had crossed the river in thousands, mostly on foot, and had taken the General in flank and rear, while others annoyed him by a galling fire from across the river.

Hemmed in on all sides, the troops fought steadily, but the fire of the enemy was so close and rapid that they melted like snow before it, and fell dead among their horses in heaps. He could not tell how long the fight lasted, but it took considerable time to kill all the soldiers. The firing was continued until the last man of Custer's command was dead. Several other bodies besides that of Custer remained unscalped, because the warriors had grown weary of the slaughter. The watercourse, in which most of the soldiers died, ran with blood.[5] He had seen many massacres, but nothing to equal that.

If the troops had not been encumbered by their horses, which plunged, reared, and kicked under the appalling fire of the Sioux, they might have done better. As it was, a great number of Indians fell, the soldiers using their revolvers at close range with deadly effect. More Indians died by the pistol than by the carbine. The latter weapon was always faulty.

---

[5]This, of course, is an exaggerated figure of speech. By Horned Horse's own account, only "several" of Custer's troopers were wounded in the river.

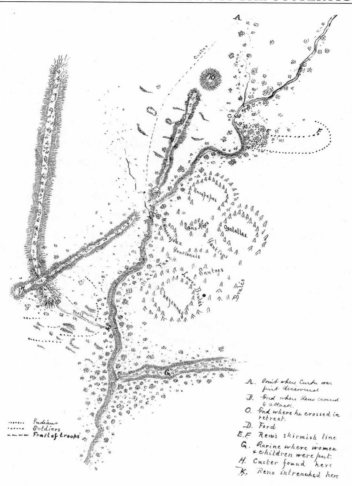

A. Point where Custer was
     first discovered
B. Ford where Reno crossed
     to attack
C. Ford where he crossed in
     retreat.
D. Ford.
E.F Reno's skirmish line
G. Ravine where women
     & children were put.
H. Custer found here
K. Reno intrenched here

········ Indians
········ Soldiers
– – – – Trail of troops

It "leaded" easily and the cartridge shells stuck in the breech
the moment it became heated, owing to some defect in the
ejector.... [6]

---

[6]The facts contradict this statement. A laboratory analysis of recovered cartridge
cases from Custer's battlefield indicated extraction failure with only 3 of 69 identified
carbines. The extraction failure on Reno Hill was 4 out of 60 identified carbines. This
means that roughly 5 of every 100 troopers may have experienced extraction problems
with the Springfield carbine.

The White Bull, Brave Wolf, and Hump Narrative

Editorial note: The White Bull, Brave Wolf, and Hump narrative is contained in the military report of Lt. Oscar F. Long, Fifth U.S. Infantry, dated June 27, 1877, of which a copy is housed with the Oscar F. Long Papers, Collection CB 939, Box 1, University of California at Berkeley, California. It is reproduced hereafter with their permission.

White Bull (1834–1910) was one of the most respected shamans among the Northern Cheyennes. He acquired the healing powers of the bear, the antelope, and the wild hog, and was instructed by the Thunder Beings in the making of several protective war bonnets, including the bonnet worn by the celebrated warrior Roman Nose. After the surrender of the Cheyennes, White Bull enlisted as an Indian Scout and served under Col. Nelson A. Miles in the campaign against Lame Deer's Minneconjous and the Nez Perces. For additional interviews with White Bull, see Hardorff, *Cheyenne Memories*, pp. 37–40 and 79–81.

Brave Wolf (1820–1910) was the son of Horn who was a famous prophet among the Northern Cheyennes. Brave Wolf was married to Corn Woman who was the sister of Chief

Crazy Head. After Corn Woman left him, Brave Wolf vowed to become a Contrary, and from 1866 until 1876 he lived a life of solitary hardships. Upon the surrender of the Cheyennes, he enlisted as an Indian Scout and served under Col. Nelson A. Miles in the campaigns against Lame Deer and Chief Joseph. For another interview with Brave Wolf, see ibid, pp. 33–36.

Hump (1847–1908) was the son of the Minneconjou leader Dog's Necklace and a Cheyenne woman. After Hump's surrender in March of 1877, he enlisted as an Indian Scout and served under Col. Nelson A. Miles in the campaigns against the hostiles. Hump was severely wounded in the Bear Paw Fight against the Nez Perces. Out of admiration for Col. Miles, Hump named his three sons after the military commander, namely Nelson Hump, William Miles Hump, and John Bear Coat Hump. For additional information about Hump, see his 1881 interview which is printed herein.

The report which follows contains information obtained by Lt. Oscar F. Long, Acting Engineer Officer, from enlisted Indian Scouts during an excursion to Custer Battlefield with Col. Nelson A. Miles and units of the Fifth Infantry.

Custer Battlefield, Montana Territory
June 27, 1878

The Indian force was composed of six tribes: The Uncpapas under Sitting Bull, Ogallallas under Crazy Horse, Minneconjoux under Lame Deer,[1] Sans Arcs under Roan Bear,[2]

---

[1]Lame Deer was a renowned Minneconjou Shirt Wearer who was treated by his people with the same respect as a hereditary chief. Being a traditionalist, he renounced reservation life and refused to surrender. Lame Deer was killed on present Lame Deer Creek, Montana, on May 7, 1877, by troops under Gen. Nelson A. Miles. After the battle, one of Lame Deer's three sons, Flying By, returned to recover his father's body, but found it decapitated, the trunk containing seventeen bullet wounds.

[2]Roan Bear, or Red Bear, was the leader of a Northern Sans Arc band who surrendered in March of 1877. He enlisted in the U.S. Indian Scouts with the rank of Sergeant and was a member of the Oglala delegation which visited Washington, D.C., in 1877.

Cheyennes under Little Wolf,[3] and one small tribe of disaffected Indians from Spotted Tail Agency. This last [group] numbered about twenty fighting men who were encamped at the upper end of the village, on the left bank of the Little Big Horn.[4]

The cavalry was first seen by some squaws who were about seven miles distant from their village, digging roots and gathering herbs. These squaws were mounted on ponies and, being chased by the soldiers, hastened back to the Indian village and gave the alarm, one of them being overtaken and killed in the flight.[5]

This was the first intimation the Indians had of the presence of the soldiers. The actual number of Indians cannot be ascertained [as] there were too many lodges to be counted. The Indians saw General Terry's command coming up the Little Big Horn about noon the day after the fight, and

---

[3]Little Wolf (1821–1904) was a respected Cheyenne tribal chief and a man who had much influence over his people. He had once been the head soldier of the Elk Society and as such had gained a reputation of a dominant leader. He was a member of the Cheyenne delegation which visited Washington, D.C., in 1873. Little Wolf did not partake in the Custer Battle, having arrived too late from Red Cloud Agency. However, he was wounded six times during the destruction of Dull Knife's village in November of 1876. After the relocation of the Cheyennes in Indian Territory, Little Wolf led his band on an epic journey to their northern homeland in Montana and surrendered at Ft. Keogh in 1879.

[4]Since these individuals were from Spotted Tail Agency, we may assume that they were Brule Lakotas. The term that they were "disaffected Indians" is puzzling because in essence the entire village was disaffected, including a Brule camp of sixty-five lodges located near the Oglalas. The camp of the twenty Spotted Tail Indians at the upper end of the village may have been tribal traders (Brule Loafers) who were disaffected with the Northern bands. Evidence suggests that some of their ponies were stolen and that they were treated with contempt by the camp police of the Northern bands. They may have been the same people who discovered Custer's bivouac on Davis Creek early on June 25 and who returned to the village to strike the alarm.

[5]These women were fired upon by Ree Scouts—Little Sioux, Red Star, Strikes Two, and Boy Chief—who were operating in the valley ahead of Reno's advancing battalion. After the battle, burial details found the bodies of six women in a little ravine in front of Reno's skirmish line. Although the Rees later denied their complicity in the slayings, George Herendeen was emphatic in his statement that the killings had been done by Indian Scouts and not by the soldiers.

immediately moved up the valley of a small branch of the Little Big Horn River.[6] Custer rode down quite close to the river, but did not attempt to cross.

The [Reno] fight commenced about 11 A.M. and ended a little before 12 P.M. One soldier's horse became unmanageable and carried him through the Indian village and ten miles beyond, when his horse gave out and he was killed.[7] There were several soldiers in the fight who, seeing no escape, shot themselves.

When Custer and his men first saw the village, they gave three cheers.[8] At that season of the year, the river could have been forded almost anywhere with little or no difficulty, the water being very low. About twenty Arapahoes joined Sitting Bull soon after General Crook's fight with the Indians and came very near being killed, for the Indians thought they were spies and had been scouting for the soldiers.[9]

While Custer was making his last stand on the hill, about forty of his men, letting their horses loose, made a break from the command and endeavored to reach the timber on the Little Big Horn, but none succeeded [and] all were killed.[10] No officer was with these soldiers. The Indians could not distinguish an officer from a soldier. As soon as a man would fall, the Indians would rush up and scalp him. The [soldier] hors-

---

[6]This branch was Shoulder Blade Creek, known to the Lakotas as Box Elder Creek or Bird Timber Creek, just west of present Garryowen, Montana.

[7]This may have been Pvt. George A. Smith (1850–1876) of M Company. Smith rode a hardmouthed horse which bolted from the skirmish line and ran straight into the Indian village, never to be seen again.

[8]The cheering heard by the Indians is confirmed by Trumpeter John Martin and two of Custer's Crow scouts, Curley and White Man Runs Him, who stated that the troops cheered after Custer waved his hat while viewing the sprawling village from the bluffs.

[9]Actually there were only five Arapahoes, namely Left Hand, Yellow Eagle, Waterman, Yellow Fly, and Green Grass, also known as Well Knowing One. This Arapaho war party had left Fort Robinson on a foray against the Shoshones, but was discovered and detained by the Sioux who suspected them to be army scouts. Through the intervention of the Cheyennes—particularly Two Moons who had Arapaho relatives—the five captives were released and subsequently took part in the Custer Battle.

es or the men did not seem to be tired. Custer did not try to cross the river. He first made a stand about 800 yards from the river, [but] then fell back as the Indians increased in numbers to where he made his final stand.

They saw Reno when he was coming down the valley of the small creek at the upper end of the village. He crossed the river above the mouth of this creek, [and] charged (horseback) down the valley and through the upper end of the Uncpapa village—these Indians ran toward Crazy Horse's village. Reno soon after deployed as skirmishers across the valley, below the wood, but soon after was driven back to the wood—coming out of the wood again, [he] once more was driven back and remained there but a short time. Twenty of Reno's men made a break for the river and endeavored to reach the pack train on the opposite side, [but] only five were successful.[11]

Lt. McIntosh was killed a short distance from the wood where Reno [had] made his stand.[12] Reno and his command

---

[10]This total is corroborated by the Cheyenne Two Moons who added that five of these men were mounted. According to the Oglala, He Dog, the dismounted soldiers ran to Deep Ravine, while the mounted ones tried to escape south toward Calhoun Ridge.

[11]The retreat route used by most of Reno's troopers curved along the south side of the river bends to the retreat crossing. However, a sketch map by Lt. Long (not reproduced herein) reveals that a bunch of twenty soldiers retreated along an alternative route across a loop in the river, forcing them to cross the water three times before reaching the east bank of the Little Bighorn. This loop is the southern most loop, or bend, from present Garryowen, its curve laying just west of the retreat crossing. According to Indian witnesses, fifteen soldiers of this bunch of twenty were slain on the alternative route. Of the thirty-two enlisted men killed during the retreat, the approximate kill sites of twenty-four are known, leaving eight as yet to be determined. The majority of these missing men belonged to G Company who may have been slain along the alternative route. On June 28 a burial party found seven bodies on a shallow sandbar in the southern loop of the alternative route.

[12]Lt. Donald McIntosh (1838–1876) commanded G Company of Reno's battalion and was killed during the retreat from the valley. Not being able to find his orderly who held his horse, McIntosh took the mount of Pvt. Samuel McCormick without first removing a loosened picket pin. This pin bounced around at the end of a dragging lariat, which annoyed the horse and impeded his gait, and may have caused the death of McIntosh. His remains were horribly mutilated and were identified only through a gutta-percha button torn from the shirt worn by the victim. McIntosh was buried by the 7th Infantry on June 27.

retreated from the wood, forded the river and gained the hill, [the Indians stating] they run like a herd of buffalo. Lieut. Hodgson was killed while trying to cross the river with Reno, [and] they succeeded in getting his two pistols and watch.[13]

Almost all the Indians who were killed in the fight were killed by Custer's command. Reno's command killed seven Indians.[14] Altogether thirty-eight Indians were killed in the fight. An officer was killed where Custer made his first stand—nearest the river. This officer had a pair of field glasses and a compass (wooden box).

If Reno had held his position in the wood, the Indians could not have driven him out, but they would have been obliged to have left. It was a good place for defense, [with] plenty of water and trees, and he (Reno) ought to have remained.

Many of Custer's men were found with belts full (or nearly so) of ammunition, and many of the captured horses were found with saddle bags attached and in the bags was plenty of ammunition. One company started to run when Custer was near the river and the rest [of the battalion] fired on them and made them come back. This was the Bay Horse Company, probably Keogh's.[15]

---

[13]Benjamin H. Hodgson was a second lieutenant in B Company, but was assigned to Reno's battalion to serve as its adjutant. Hodgson was killed on the east bank of the river, some twenty feet from the water. His naked body contained a gunshot wound in the temple, inflicted at close range, and another one in the groin, just below the belt line. The body was slashed and a single arrow was sticking from it. Hodgson's remains were buried on the bluffs near the entrenchments of B Company on the morning of June 27. His gold watch case was later recovered from the Indians.

[14]The Indian loss sustained during the valley fight amounted to twenty people, among them six women and four children. Of the ten warriors killed, two were Cheyennes, Roman Nose and Whirlwind, and eight were Sioux, Dog with Horns, Young Black Moon, Hawk Man, White Buffalo, Chased by Owls, White Eagle, Elk Stand Above, and Three Bears.

[15]Three of the five companies with Custer rode bay horses, namely F, I, and L. These five companies were divided into two battalions, consisting of E and F Companies commanded by Capt. George Yates, and I, L, and C Companies under Capt. Myles Keogh. Students of the battle have generally accepted the theory that Yates' battalion operated near the river before being ordered back to the heights by Custer. This retreat maneuver was probably executed under cover fire by Keogh's battalion, which may have been mistaken by the Indians as to its intent.

It is not known where Lieut. Sturgis was killed, but [he was] probably with Custer or Calhoun.[16] The Minneconjoux Sioux captured a black iron-gray horse with a saddle blanket with yellow stripes around it, having killed the officer who rode him. A trumpeter, with [his] trumpet [hanging] on his back, was the last man killed in the fight.[17] No white man was in the Indian camp at the time of the fight. No soldiers were taken prisoner. No wounded men were taken [prisoner]; they always kill the men.[18]

If two or three pieces of artillery had been on the hill where Custer was and had opened fire on the Indian village, the Indians would have become demoralized and would have run, for they are very much afraid of large guns. As Reno was crossing the river just previous to taking his final position on the hill, the Indians saw Custer on the bluffs on the opposite side of the river, and most of them, leaving Reno, forded the river and went after Custer, who had his men dismounted on the ridge on which they were killed. Custer did not attempt to cross for the Indians had [already] crossed before he could possibly have forded the river, and, gaining a small hill on the north side of the Little Big Horn, [the Indians] placed themselves between Custer and the river.

Calhoun's company, leaving the command and charging down the ridge on the hill where the Indians were, drove them before him, but soon after was surrounded and all [were] killed. Five guidons were captured. All the Indians

---

[16]Lt. James E. Sturgis was regularly assigned to M Company, but was transferred to E Company at the outset of the campaign. He was declared MIA and presumed killed. A decapitated and scorched head found in the Indian village by a member of the burial details was thought to have resembled that of Sturgis.

[17]This unfortunate victim may have been Pvt. Henry C. Dose (1849–1876) of G Company who was assigned to headquarters staff as Custer's trumpeter orderly. He was laying facedown on the south bank of Deep Ravine, near the river, his mutilated body riddled with arrows in the sides and back. Dose rode a grey horse and was listed as a sharpshooter.

[18]This statement is contradicted by the Hunkpapa Little Knife whose interview follows hereafter.

thought Custer a brave man [because] he did not run; but Reno ran [and] he was not a brave man—he was not a man at all but a squaw, else he would have come down to the aid of Custer.

If Reno had come [to Custer's battlefield] his soldiers would have followed him. If Reno had joined Custer, there would have been too many soldiers for the Indians. Reno and Custer together could have held the ridge, and Custer and his command would not all have been killed. Reno should have come down when the Indians first went after Custer—followed them across [the river], and then he (Reno) could have joined Custer, for the Indians would [then] have been between two fires, and Custer would have been saved. Reno could have come down the valley and could have crossed the river for he had but little opposition from the Indians, and Custer would have seen him coming and probably [would] have continued on instead of falling back to the high ridge where he was killed.

As far as the Indians know, there was no communication between Reno and Custer after the fight commenced.[19] The Indians all rushed after Custer together—it is not known which tribe first engaged him. When first seen by the Indians, Custer and his command were nearly all on foot, only a few being mounted, and all were hastening toward that point where Custer fell. The reason assigned to Custer's not crossing the river is that he probably saw too many Indians in his front.

Custer and his men fought well—they were brave soldiers; they fired well; [and] they did not appear frightened. Eleven men and one squaw from Spotted Tail Agency started from the Indian camp to go back to their agency, but, seeing

---

[19]Pvt. Archibald McIlhargey and Pvt. John E. Mitchell, both of I Company but assigned to Reno's staff, were dispatched by Reno with a message to Custer at the outset of the valley fight. Neither man was ever seen alive again.

Custer's command (before it was divided), [they] returned to the Indian village and gave warning.[20]

Sitting Bull and Crazy Horse were the greatest chiefs among the Sioux. Sitting Bull had one pony shot under him, [and] Crazy Horse two. One soldier started to run back on the trail, but being cut off, [he] jumped in a ravine and shot himself.[21] The Sauntee [Santee] (Cut Heads) shot Custer and captured his bald-faced sorrel horse.[22] The Sioux knew Custer and called him the Long Haired Chief.

The above disconnected facts, elicited from the Indians, are given as nearly verbatim as possible.

---

[20]This party consisted of only seven agency Indians, identified as Black Bear, Owl Bull, Medicine Bird, Blue Cloud, Kills Enemy in Winter, Knife, and the latter's wife who had eloped with him on June 24. It is further known that they were Oglalas en route to Red Cloud Agency. This Lakota party was joined by three Cheyennes, Big Crow, Black Horse, and Medicine Bull, who were scouts from Little Wolf's camp of forty Cheyennes who followed in the rear of Custer's column. It is possible, therefore, that these three Cheyennes remained with the Lakotas and hurried to the village to strike the alarm. Black Bear was later interviewed by Walter Camp and denied that his party returned to the village.

[21]This may have been Cpl. John Foley (1850–1876) who fled Custer Hill at the end of the battle and who shot himself on the rise between Deep Coulee and Medicine Tail Coulee, some 400 yards from the river.

[22]On June 25 Custer rode Vic, a Kentucky thoroughbred of chestnut color which had a blaze in the face and three white fetlocks. This gelding, which was nicknamed Peep of Day by the soldiers, was allegedly captured by a Santee named Sounds the Ground as He Walks who was Red Top's oldest son.

The Little Knife Interview

Editorial note: The Little Knife interview is contained in a feature article published in the *Billings Gazette*, partially dated 1926, of which a clipping is housed in the Billings Clipping File, Billings Public Library, Montana. A subject search failed to disclose any information on this Hunkpapa eyewitness.

[Woody Mountain, Canada]
[Summer, 1879]

The memory of the [Custer] battle was still fresh in the minds of the Indians who took part in it. The story told in the summer of 1879 in the camp of the Uncapapas in the Wood Mountain region of southern Canada, and assented to by three or four warriors who corroborated each other, is to the effect that General Custer was killed by a lad of 15 years of age.

The General was cheering his men and firing his pistol in the air—the cavalry signal to charge—it was stated. From the start he was in advance of his command. When he fell he was between the Indians on horseback and his own flying squadron. While trying to restore some order in his broken ranks, a stray shot killed a young buck not far from General Custer's position. The dead warrior's brother, an Indian lad 15 years of age, seized his brother's gun and shot Custer dead, according to the Wood Mountain recital.

The boy was still in the camp in the Wood Mountain country and he carried a coup stick in which there was a deep notch to represent the taking-off of one of the best Indian fighters the Plain ever knew. After the battle, for a brief period, the Indians gathered around the body of "Long Hair," as they called the General, and loud and jubilant was the requiem sung over the dead soldier. . . .

Little Knife said that as soon as the soldiers struck camp and the battle opened, the Indians saw that they had an inferior force to contend with. The men were poor riders and, according to Little Knife, were easily shaken from their horses. In firing their carbines and later their pistols they were wild, and in retreating they fired over their shoulders, killing their own comrades as they went. Both horses and men appeared to be unmanageable from the outset, he said, and they fell a prey to the steady firing of the Indian enemy and the careless and reckless shooting among themselves. Some who were thrown from their horses approached the Indians with their hands up, but they were shot down.

One prisoner was taken. He was captured by Rain-in-the-Face, who said he had stripes on his arm. The prisoner was undoubtedly Corporal Ryan. He was bound hand and foot with a "shag-a-nappe" (stripped buffalo hide), and left in a lodge. A wild dance followed in the night after the battle, and a few men, drunk with the excitement of the results of the conflict, sought out the lodge in which the captive was held and killed him with a knife. . . .[1]

---

[1]A similar statement was made by the Cheyenne, Two Moons, who admitted that some of the soldier bodies had been dragged into the village, and were dismembered and burned during the big dance held that night. On June 28, burial parties found scorched human bones and parts of blue uniforms in the village.

"Sitting Bull had very little to do with the big battle," said Little Knife. "He was on the butte (hill) on the flank of the Indian camp. Towards the close of the fight he was in the camp keeping it in order and looking after the women and children."

"Who was the chief in command?" Little Knife was asked.

"There was none," he replied. "The headmen commanded the men under them, but there was no general chief."

"How many did the Indians lose?" he was asked.

The old chief named each one of the Indian casualties and counted them on his fingers. "There were 32 Indians actually killed," he said.

"How many soldiers?"

"I can't say; a great many."

"Did your people get many trophies?" Little Knife was asked.

"We got seven hundred guns and pistols. We also got two horns (bugles) and a flag," he replied.

It was observed in the Indian camp that almost every Uncapapa was armed with a breech loading carbine that was taken off the battlefield. No trace of the bugles was found. The standard was made up into a shirt for one of the young bucks who wore it with the red and white stripes running perpendicular and the blue field of stars hanging over his back.[2]

Little Knife was asked if any scalps were taken.

"No, not one," he replied. "We scalped nobody; we came away as fast as we could."

"How many soldiers did you kill?" was asked directly of the Uncapapa chief.

---

[2]This was neither the regimental standard, which was not displayed on June 25, nor Custer's personal flag, which did not have any stars. The latter flag was a large swallow-tailed guidon, divided into a red and a blue field, with white crossed sabres in the center. Most likely the "standard" spoken of was a swallow-tailed company guidon, two by three feet in size, containing yellow stars on a small blue field, bordered by horizontal red and white stripes.

"None; I never killed a white man in my life. I have only killed Crow Indians." Little Knife is believed to have perjured himself in that reply.

"Are you on the warpath now with the Americans?"

"No," replied Little Knife, "I am a warrior. My heart is strong; I am brave, but I don't want war. I am tired of fighting. I am not willing to go back to my country, even if the Americans will let me. I don't want to give up my guns and horses. I want to hunt; but I will hurt no man unless he hurts me."

The Hump Interview

Editorial note: The Hump interview is contained in a newspaper despatch forwarded from Ft. Yates on July 30, 1881, and printed in the *Leavenworth Times,* Sunday issue of August 14, 1881, of which a clipping is in the author's collection.

Hump (1847–1908), also known as High Back Bone and Big Chest '*Canku Wakantuya*,' was one of the most influential band leaders among the Minneconjou Sioux in 1881 and had a larger following than any of the other Northern Sioux chiefs. It was said among the Minneconjous that he had once captured a Thunder Bird. Hump took his uncle's name in 1870 when the latter was killed during a raiding party against the Shoshones. Hump had two brothers named Little Crow and Iron Thunder. The latter's account of the battle is printed hereafter. Hump died on the Cheyenne River Reservation in November of 1908, having been blind the last decade of his life. The identity of the reporter is not known. The account which follows has been divided into paragraphs.

[Fort Yates, Dakota Territory]
[July 30, 1881]

The sun was about at meridian when the fight began. That was the first we knew that the white warriors were coming.

They attacked the Uncpapas first. They were at the upper end of our camp. The Minnicongoes, Sausaves [Sans Arcs] and Cheyennes were near the center of the camp, but nearer the end of the camp furthest from where the attack was made. The charge was from the upper end of the camp. The Indians gave way slowly, retreating until they got their horses and got mounted. Just as soon as they got sufficient force— for our warriors were rushing to help them as fast as they could—they drove the white warriors back, and they retreat- ed. These were Reno's men.

I had a horse that I could not manage. He was not mine, and was not well broke; so I went to where the horses were, and the women and the old men and boys were gathering them together, and caught a horse that I could manage bet- ter, and when I had caught him and mounted, the other party of white warriors (Custer's forces) charged. The Indians had by that time all got together, and it seemed, the way Custer came, that he started to cut off our retreat, not appearing to know where Reno was, or that he had retreated.

When the Indians charged on the long-haired chief and his men, the long-haired chief and his men became confused, and they retreated slowly, but it was no time at all before the Indians had the long-haired chief and his men surrounded. Then our chiefs gave the "hi-yi-yi" yell, and all the Indians joined, and they whipped each other's horses, and they made such short work of killing them, that no man could give any correct account of it. The first charge the Indians made they never slacked up or stopped. They made a finish of it. The Indians and whites were so mixed up that you could hardly tell anything about it.

[During] the first dash the Indians made my horse was shot from under me and I was wounded—shot above the knee, and the ball came out at the hip (here the interpreter said that he had seen the scar), and I fell and lay right there.[1] The rest of the Indians kept on horseback, and I did not get in the final fight. It was a clear day. There was no storm nor thunder nor lightning. The report was that it was the long-haired chief that came to fight us, but that was all we knew.

I know that Sitting Bull was in the fight, but on account of my wound I did not know anything he did. Every able-bodied Indian there took part in the fight, as far as I could tell. Those that did not join in the fight, it was because they could not find room to get in. There was a good many agency Indians in our camp. They all took part in the fight, same as the hostiles. The agency Indians had come out, and all made report to us that Long Hair was coming to fight us. So the Indians all got together that he might not strike small parties, and not for the purpose of fighting or counseling [against] Long Hair [and] what he was coming for, but, [rather], they were getting ready to be strong to defend themselves.

---

[1]It appears from Hump's description that he was wounded at Calhoun Hill, where troops under Lt. James Calhoun fought a gallant fight, accounting for a considerable number of Indian casualties on Custer's battlefield.

The Iron Thunder Interview

Editorial note: The Iron Thunder Interview is contained in a newspaper despatch forwarded from Fort Yates on July 30, 1881, and printed in the *Leavenworth Times*, Sunday issue of August 14, 1881, of which a clipping is in the author's collection.

Iron Thunder was a Minneconjou Lakota who was born about 1848. He was a brother of Chief Hump and Little Crow. The identity of the reporter is not known. The account which follows has been divided into paragraphs.

[Fort Yates, Dakota Territory]
[July 30, 1881]

We were encamped on the west side of the Little Big Horn. On the upper side of the camp was a small ash grove, and the camp was strung along from that grove more than two miles down the river. The camps were close together, one band adjoining another all the way down.

I did not know anything about Reno's attack until his men were so close that the bullets went through the camp, and everything was in confusion. The horses were so frightened we could not catch them. I was catching any horse to join in the fight. When I caught him and was mounted, our warriors had driven the white men off and were running after them.

Then I followed the way they went, and I saw a lot of horse-men—Indians—crossing the river, and went after them.

I followed them across the river, and before I overtook them, going up the hill, I found an Indian lying there dead. I knew him. He and I were sworn friends. I stopped to look at him.[1] The whites were still firing back at us. Just as I arrived where our men were, the report came to us that another party was coming to attack us. We could not see them from where we were. The report was that they were coming to head off the women and children from the way they were going, and so we turned around and went towards them. Our men moved around in the direction of a circle, but I cut across to a knoll and looked up the river and saw them coming down.[2]

The day before the fight I had come back from a war party against the Crows. I had only one horse, and his feet were worn out (the Indians do not shoe their horses, and they often give out on long marches), and by the time I got half-way back to where Long-Haired Chief and his men were my horse was so lame I could go no further. I was nearly two miles away when the Indians charged Long-Haired Chief and his warriors. You could not notice the difference in [the position of] the sun from the time Custer was charged until he was done away with. Agency Indians, Yanktons and San-tees were there. All took part. Every Indian took part in the fight that could. But there was such confusion that no one could tell the particulars of what was done.

---

[1]Iron Thunder's statement about the slain Lakota suggests a bond formed through the *Hunka Lowanpi*, a ceremony in which one person ritually adopts another one. These individuals were called *hunka*. They were allowed to wear a red stripe on the face and were expected to sacrifice their lives for each other. Although Iron Thunder does not reveal the identity of the dead man, we know that the victim was one of only two Lakota casualties who died on the east side of the river. One was a Sans Arc head soldier of one of the military lodges who was slain by Rees on a hillock north of Reno Hill. The second casualty, and probably Iron Thunder's *hunka*, was a young Oglala named White Eagle who was killed on the slope of Reno Hill while pursuing the retreating soldiers too closely.

[2]This elevation may have been Weir Point, known to the Lakotas as Black Butte. Since it is an absolute fact that Custer was near Medicine Tail Coulee by the time Reno reached Reno Hill, Iron Thunder must have been looking *downstream* rather than *upstream*.

The Low Dog Interview

Editorial note: The Low Dog interview is contained in a newspaper despatch forwarded from Fort Yates on July 30, 1881, and printed in the *Leavenworth Times*, Sunday issue of August 14, 1881, of which a clipping is in the author's collection.

Low Dog (1847–1894) was a prominent Oglala warrior who had married a woman from the Northern Cheyenne tribe. He lost an older brother in the Custer battle, and rather than facing reservation life, he preferred sanctuary in Canada where he joined Sitting Bull's Hunkpapas. Low Dog surrendered at Camp Poplar, in present Montana, in 1881, and settled among the Minneconjous at Cheyenne River Agency. He was described as being a tall, straight man, with regular features and small hands and feet, and "not a bad face." The identity of the reporter is not known. The account which follows has been divided into paragraphs.

[Fort Yates, Dakota Territory]
[July 30, 1881]

We were in camp near [the] Little Big Horn River. We had lost some horses, and an Indian went back on the trail to look for them.[1] We did not know that the white warriors

---

[1]On June 24 a small Lakota hunting party left a worn-out pony on Spring Creek, now known as the South Fork of Reno Creek. The owner of this pony was a young

were coming after us. Some scouts or men in advance of the [white] warriors saw the Indian looking for the horses and ran after him and tried to kill him to keep him from bringing us word, but he ran faster than they and came into camp and told us that the white warriors were coming.[2]

I was asleep in my lodge at the time. The sun was about noon (pointing with his finger). I heard the alarm, but I did not believe it. I thought it was a false alarm. I did not think it possible that any white men would attack us, so strong as we were. We had in camp the Cheyennes, Arapahos, and seven different tribes of the Teton Sioux—a countless number. Although I did not believe it was a true alarm, I lost no time getting ready. When I got my gun and came out of my lodge, the attack had begun at the part of the camp where Sitting Bull and the Uncpapas were. The Indians held their ground to give the women and children time to get out of the way.

By this time the herders were driving in the horses, and as I was nearly at the further end of the camp, I ordered my men to catch their horses and mount. But there was much confusion. The women and children were trying to catch their horses and get out of the way, and my men were hurrying to go and help those that were fighting. When the fighters saw that the women and children were safe they fell back. By this time my people went to help them, and the less able warriors and women caught horses and got them ready, and we drove the first attacking party back, and that party retreated to a high hill. Then I told my people not to venture too far in pursuit for fear of falling in an ambush.

Hunkpapa boy named Deeds who went back to the Little Bighorn village, riding double with his brother Little Voice. The following morning Deeds returned to Spring Creek with his father, Little Bear, and recovered the pony. While riding near the divide, they were discovered by Lt. Charles Varnum and his scouts who tried to intercept and kill them.

[2]Deeds was mortally wounded by Custer's Indian scouts near the lower fork of Reno Creek. His father escaped and was able to alarm the Hunkpapa camp moments before Reno's attack.

By this time all the warriors in our camp were mounted and ready for fight, and then we were attacked on the other side by another party. They came on us like a thunderbolt. I never before nor since saw men so brave and fearless as those white warriors. We retreated until our men got all together, and then we charged upon them. I called to my men, "This is a good day to die: follow me." We massed our men, and that no man should fall back, every man whipped another man's horse and we rushed right upon them.[3]

As we rushed upon them the white warriors dismounted to fire, but they did very poor shooting. They held their horses' reins on one arm while they were shooting, but their horses were so frightened that they pulled the men all around, and a great many of their shots went up in the air and did us no harm. The white warriors stood their ground bravely, and none of them made any attempt to get away.

After all but two of them were killed, I captured two of their horses. Then the wise men and chiefs of our nation gave out [the advice] to our people not to mutilate the dead white chief, for he was a brave warrior and died a brave man, and his remains should be respected.

Then I turned round and went to help fight the other white warriors, who had retreated to a high hill on the east side of the river. (This was Reno's command.) I don't know whether any white men of Custer's force were taken prisoners. When I got back to our camp they were all dead.

Everything was in confusion all the time of the fight. I did not see Gen. Custer. I do not know who killed him. We did not know till the fight was over that he was the white chief. We had no idea that the white warriors were coming until the runner came in and told us. I do not say that Reno was a coward. He fought well, but our men were fighting to save their women and children, and drive them back. If Reno and

---

[3]This action took place during the final moments of the fight for Calhoun Hill.

his warriors had fought as Custer and his warriors fought, the battle might [have] been against us. No white man or Indian ever fought as bravely as Custer and his men.

The next day we fought Reno and his forces again, and killed many of them.[4] Then the chiefs said these men had been punished enough, and that we ought to be merciful, and let them go. Then we heard that another force was coming up the river to fight us (General Terry's command), and we started to fight them, but the chiefs and the wise men counseled that we had fought enough and that we should not fight unless attacked, and we went back and took our women and children and went away.

. . . Thirty-eight [Indians were killed], who died then, and a great many—I can't tell the number—who were wounded and died afterwards.[5] I never saw a fight in which so many in proportion to the killed were wounded, and [in which also] so many horses were wounded. . . . Eight were chiefs killed in the battle; one was his own brother, born of the same father and mother. . . .

---

[4]The dead toll sustained during the defense of Reno Hill amounted to eleven enlisted men and one civilian employee. Three other enlisted men later succumbed to the trauma of their wounds.

[5]Documentary evidence has revealed the names of only three warriors who died later: one Cheyenne, Cut Belly, who died on Powder River, and two Lakotas, *Wasicun Sapa* 'Black White Man,' and *Mato Yamni* 'Three Bears,' who both died on Wood Louse Creek, at the foot of the Big Horn Mountains.

The Crow King Interview

Editorial note: The Crow King Interview is contained in a newspaper despatch forwarded from Fort Yates on July 30, 1881, and printed in the *Leavenworth Times*, Sunday issue of August 14, 1881, of which a clipping is in the author's collection.

Crow King, or Patriarch Crow, was a noted warrior and the influential leader of a large Hunkpapa band. It was said among his followers that he had a quick temper and that he had once killed another Lakota in a fit of anger. He had three brothers of which two were killed during the Custer battle. Crow King was a member of the Silent Eaters Lodge. After the surrender of his band at Camp Poplar, Montana, in January 1881, he enlisted in the Standing Rock Indian Police and served until his death in 1884. The account which follows has been divided into paragraphs.

[Fort Yates, Dakota Territory]
[July 30, 1881]

We were in camp not thinking there was any danger of a battle, although we had heard that the long-haired chief had been sent after us. Some of our runners went back on our trail, for what purpose I do not know. One came back and reported that an army of white soldiers was coming, and he had no more than reported when another runner came in with the same story, and also told us that the command had divided, and that one party was going round to attack us on the opposite side.[1]

The first attack was at the camp of the Uncpapas tribe. The shots neither raised or fell. (Here he indicated that the whites commenced firing at about four hundred yards distance.) The Indians retreated—at first slowly, to give the women and children time to go to a place of safety. Other Indians got our horses. By that time we had warriors enough to turn upon the whites and we drove them to the hill, and started back to camp.

Then the second band of white warriors came. We did not know who was their chief, but we supposed it was Custer's command. The party commenced firing at long range. (Indicating nearly a mile.) We had then all our warriors and horses. There were eighty warriors in my band. All the Sioux were there from everywhere. We had warriors plenty as the leaves on the trees. Our camp was as long as from the fort to the lower end of our camp here. (More than two and a half miles.) Sitting Bull and Crazy Horse were the great chiefs of the fight. Sitting Bull did not fight himself, but he gave orders.

We turned against this second party. The greater portion of our warriors came together in their front and we rushed our horses on them. At the same time warriors rode out on each side of them and circled around them until they were surrounded. When they saw that they were surrounded they dismounted. They tried to hold on to their horses, but as we

---

[1]This is another reference to Little Bear whose son was slain during the attempt to alarm the village. The second messenger was probably sent back by the party of agency Indians who had left the Little Bighorn at dawn.

pressed closer they let go their horses. We crowded them towards our main camp and killed them all. They kept in order and fought like brave warriors as long as they had a man left.

Our camp was on Greasy Grass River. (Little Big Horn.) When we charged, every chief gave the cry, "Hi-yi-yi." (Here Crow Chief gave us the cry in a high, prolonged tone.) When this cry is given it is a command to all the warriors to watch the chief, and follow his actions. Then every chief rushed his horse on the white soldiers, and all our warriors did the same, every one whipping another's horse. There was great hurry and confusion in the fight. No one chief was above another in that fight. It was not more than half an hour after the long-haired chief attacked us before he and his men were dead.

Then we went back for the first party. We fired at them until the sun went down. We surrounded them and watched them all night, and at daylight we fought them again. We killed many of them. Then a chief from the Uncpapas called our men off. He told them those men had been punished enough; that they were fighting under orders; that we had killed the great leader and his men in the fight the day before, and we should let the rest go home. Sitting Bull gave this order. He said, "This is not my doings, nor these men's. They are fighting because they were commanded to fight. We have killed their leader. Let them go. I call on the Great Spirit to witness what I say. We did not want to fight. Long Hair sent us word that he was coming to fight us, and we had to defend ourselves and our wives and children."

If this command [by Sitting Bull] had not been given we could have cut Reno's command to pieces, as we did Custer's. No warrior knew Custer in the fight. We did not know him, dead or alive. When the fight was over the chiefs gave orders to look for the long-haired chief among the dead, but no chief with long hair could be found. (Custer had his hair cut short before starting on this march.)

Crow King said [further] that if Reno had held out until Custer came and then fought as Custer did, that they would have whipped the Indians. The Indians would then have been compelled to divide [their force] to protect their women and children, and the whites would have had the advantage. He expressed great admiration for the bravery of Custer and his men, and said that fight impressed the Indians that the whites were their superiors and it would be their destruction to keep on fighting them. Both he and Low Dog said that they did not feel that they would be blamed for the Custer fight or its results. It was war; they were attacked; Custer tried to kill them; they killed him.

Crow King said he had two brothers killed in the fight;[2] that from thirty to fifty Indians were killed, and a much larger number who were wounded, died afterward.

---

[2]Their names were Swift Bear and White Bull, Hunkpapas, who were killed on the west side of the river during the pursuit of Reno's fleeing troops.

The Red Horse Interview

Editorial note: The Red Horse interview is contained in a paper title, "Picture-Writing of the American Indians," by Garrick Mallery, published in *The Tenth Annual Report of the Bureau of Ethnology*, Washington, D.C., 1893, pp. 563–66.

The account which follows was obtained by Dr. Charles E. McChesney, U.S. Army, from Red Horse who also provided forty-two pages of ledger art, among which a map of the battlefield which is reproduced herein. A subject search failed to disclose any information on this Minneconjou eyewitness.

[Cheyenne River Agency, Dakota Territory, 1881]

Five springs ago, I, with many Sioux Indians, took down and packed up our tepees and moved from Cheyenne River to the Rosebud River, where we camped a few days; then took down and packed up our lodges and moved to the Little Bighorn River and pitched our lodges with the large camp of Sioux.

The Sioux were camped on the Little Bighorn River as follows: The lodges of the Uncpapas were pitched highest up the river under a bluff. The Santee lodges were pitched next. The Oglala's lodges were pitched next. The Brule lodges were pitched next. The Minneconjou lodges were pitched next. The Sans Arc lodges were pitched next. The Blackfeet lodges were pitched next.[1] The Cheyenne lodges were pitched next. A few Arikara Indians were among the Sioux (being without lodges of their own). Two Kettles, among the other Sioux (without lodges).

I was a Sioux chief in the council lodge. My lodge was pitched in the center of the camp. The day of the attack I and four women were a short distance from the camp digging wild turnips. Suddenly one of the women attracted my attention to a cloud of dust rising a short distance from camp. I soon saw that the soldiers were charging the camp. To the camp I and the women ran. When I arrived a person told me to hurry to the council lodge. The soldiers charged so quickly we could not talk (council). We came out of the council lodge and talked in a all directions: ["]Sioux mount horses, take guns, and go fight the soldiers. Women and children mount horses and go,["] meaning to get out of the way.

Among the soldiers was an officer who rode a horse with four white feet. The Sioux have for a long time fought many brave men of different people, but the Sioux say this officer was the bravest man they had ever fought. I don't know whether this was Gen. Custer or not. Many of the Sioux men that I hear talking tell me it was. I saw this officer in the fight many times, but did not see his body. It has been told that he was killed by a Santee Indian, who took his horse. This officer wore a large-brimmed hat and a deerskin coat. This officer saved the lives of many soldiers by turning his horse and covering the retreat. [The] Sioux say this officer was the bravest man they ever fought.[2] I saw two officers looking alike, both having long yellowish hair.[3]

---

[1]According to the Hunkpapa, Pretty Buffalo Woman, and other sources, the Blackfeet camped with the Hunkpapas and had erected their lodges on the southern side of the Hunkpapa circle.

---

[2]In memoranda submitted with the account, Dr. McChesney stated that the brave soldier spoken of by Red Horse was Capt. Thomas French of M Company. French himself thought so too, because in an 1880 letter he mentioned his skill as a marksman, boasting to have shot eleven Indians during the retreat, stating, "I don't wonder old Red Horse thought me a spirit from the bad place." However, the soldier referred to by Red Horse was known as The Man Who Rode the Horse with Four White Feet. French, to the contrary, rode a grey horse without markings, a buffalo horse which was killed on Reno Hill on June 25. The horse with the stockings, however, was said to have been captured by a Santee named Noisy Walking, the son of Old Red Top.

In regards to Gen. Custer's apparel, it should be noted that both he and his brother Tom wore a buckskin suit and a grey, large-brimmed slouch hat with a low crown. This appears to be corroborated by the Hunkpapa, Iron Hawk, who claimed to have seen two men on Custer Hill who both wore such garments. In fact, many Indians believed that General Custer must have been one of the buckskin-clad men slain on Custer Hill. One Indian, Standing Bear, who had taken a buckskin jacket from one of the dead men, kept it hidden for many years until his mother finally destroyed it for fear of being caught with the incriminating evidence.

The Indians' conception of a Custer fully clad in buckskin has been perpetuated through the artistic renditions of many artists. This visualization seemed to have gained acceptance among a number of scholars of the battle. However, a careful scrutiny of the evidence seems to suggest the opposite to be true. Custer may have worn a buckskin outfit on June 25, but so did *both* of his brothers, Tom and Boston, while at least five other officers who were slain with the General wore buckskin jackets. It is true that a melancholy reflection by Custer's longtime orderly, John Burkman, reveals an image of Custer wearing a white hat, fringed buckskin coat, and a red tie, at noon on June 25. However sequential evidence about Custer's apparel seems to suggest a different picture. One source of information is provided by the Ree scout Soldier who told Walter Camp that Custer had taken off his buckskin coat and had tied it behind him on his horse. There can be no doubt that this observation was made hours after Burkman's observation because it occurred near the lower forks of Reno Creek.

The validity of Soldier's statement receives a boost from Lt. Charles A. DeRudio who attested to having seen both General Custer and Lt. Cooke near Reno Hill, the identification made possible by their clothing—a blue shirt and buckskin pants—the only officers who wore such a combination. Moreover, Pvt. Peter Thompson, a survivor from C Company, gained his last view of Custer north of Reno Hill, and remembered that the General was dressed in a blue shirt and buckskin pants, and that his buckskin jacket was fastened to the rear of his saddle. We may conclude from these corroborating sources that the clothing pillaged from Custer's body consisted of a blue shirt and fringed buckskin pants, and that the officer with the "large-brimmed hat and deerskin coat" was not General Custer, but may have been his brother, Capt. Thomas W. Custer. According to George Bird Grinnell, a Cheyenne named Little Horse stripped a soldier on Custer Hill who wore a buckskin coat, high boots, a red handkerchief tied around the neck, and a tattoo on the wrist, and that victim's head was smashed by enraged Sioux women—all of which fits the description of Tom Custer quite well.

[3]This may be a reference to George and Tom Custer, although both wore their hair cropped short on the campaign.

Before the attack the Sioux were camped on the Rosebud River. [The] Sioux moved down a river running into the Little Bighorn River, crossed the Little Bighorn River, and camped on its west bank. This day [of June 25] a Sioux man started to go to Red Cloud agency, but when he had gone a short distance from camp he saw a cloud of dust rising and turned back and said he thought a herd of buffalo was coming near the village.[4]

The day was hot. In a short time the soldiers charged the camp. The soldiers came on the trail made by the Sioux camp in moving, and crossed the Little Bighorn River above where the Sioux crossed, and attacked the lodges of the Uncpapas, farthest up the river. The women and children ran down the Little Bighorn River a short distance, into a ravine. The soldiers set fire to the lodges. All the Sioux now charged the soldiers and drove them in confusion across the Little Bighorn River, which was very rapid, and several soldiers were drowned in it. On a hill the soldiers stopped and the Sioux surrounded them. A Sioux man came and said that a different party of soldiers had [taken] all the women and children [as] prisoners. Like a whirlwind the word went around, and the Sioux all heard it and left the soldiers on the hill and went quickly to save the women and children.

From the hill the [Reno] soldiers were on, to the place where the different soldiers [of Custer's command] were seen, was level ground, with the exception of a creek. [The] Sioux thought the [Reno] soldiers on the hill would charge them in rear, but when they did not, the Sioux thought the soldiers on the hill were out of cartridges. As soon as we had

----

[4]On June 25 a lone Sioux hunter had killed a stray buffalo on the upper reaches of Reno Creek. While skinning this animal, he noticed dust clouds rising above the divide. Being unaware of Custer's column advancing on the east side of the divide, he mistook the dust clouds for an approaching buffalo herd and hurried back to the village to organize a communal hunt with the other members of his camp. The skinned buffalo was later found by the troops, further increasing Custer's fear that he had been discovered and that the Indians had commenced to scatter.

killed all the different soldiers [of Custer's command], the Sioux all went back to kill the soldiers on the hill. All the Sioux watched around the hill on which were the soldiers until a Sioux man came and said many walking soldiers [infantry] were coming near.[5] The coming of the walking soldiers was the saving of the soldiers on the hill. [The] Sioux can not fight the walking soldiers, being afraid of them, so the Sioux hurriedly left.

The soldiers charged the Sioux camp about noon. The soldiers were divided, one party charging right into the camp. After driving these soldiers across the river, the Sioux charged the different soldiers [Custer's command] below, and drove them in confusion; these soldiers became foolish, many throwing away their guns and raising their hands, saying, "Sioux, pity us; take us prisoners." The Sioux did not take a single soldier prisoner, but killed all of them; none were left alive for even a few minutes. These different soldiers [Custer's command] discharged their guns but little. I took a gun and two belts off two dead soldiers; out of one belt two cartridges were gone, out of the other five.

The Sioux took the guns and cartridges off the dead soldiers and went to the hill on which the [Reno] soldiers were, [and] surrounded and fought them with the guns and cartridges of the dead soldiers. Had the soldiers not divided, I think they would have killed many Sioux. The different soldiers [Custer's command] that the Sioux killed made five different stands. Once the Sioux charged right in the midst of the different soldiers and scattered them all, fighting among the soldiers hand to hand.[6]

---

[5]This was Gen. Alfred H. Terry and the Montana Column, consisting of units of the Second Cavalry and the Seventh Infantry. Their bivouac on June 26 was near the present site of Crow Agency, Montana, only a few miles north of Custer's Battlefield.

[6]This action may have taken place on the east side of Custer Ridge and probably involved Capt. Myles Keogh's I Company.

One band of soldiers [of Custer's command] was in the rear of the Sioux. When this band of soldiers charged, the Sioux fell back, and the Sioux and the soldiers stood facing each other. Then all the Sioux became brave and charged the soldiers. The Sioux went but a short distance before they separated and surrounded the soldiers. I could see the officers riding in front of the soldiers and hear them shouting [commands]. Now the Sioux had many killed. The soldiers killed 136 and wounded 160 Sioux.[7] The Sioux killed all these different soldiers [of Custer's command] in the ravine.[8]

The soldiers charged the Sioux camp farthest up the river. A short time after, the different soldiers charged the village below. While the different soldiers and Sioux were fighting together the Sioux chief said, "Sioux men, go watch the [Reno] soldiers on the hill and prevent their joining the different soldiers." The Sioux men took the clothing off the dead and dressed themselves in it. Among the soldiers were white men who were not soldiers. The Sioux, dressed in the soldiers' and white men's clothing, fought the soldiers on the [Reno] hill.

The banks of the Little Bighorn River were high, and the Sioux killed many of the [Reno] soldiers while crossing. The soldiers on the hill dig up the ground [to make trenches], and the soldiers and Sioux fought at long range, sometimes the Sioux charging close up. The fight continued at long range until a Sioux man saw the walking solders coming. When the walking soldiers came near, the Sioux became afraid and ran away.

---

[7]The dead count of 136 Indians is overstated by 100, which may have resulted from a recording or transcribing error, rather than being an intentional inflation.

[8]The ravine mentioned by Red Horse may be the hollow on the east side of Custer Ridge, where I Company was slain.

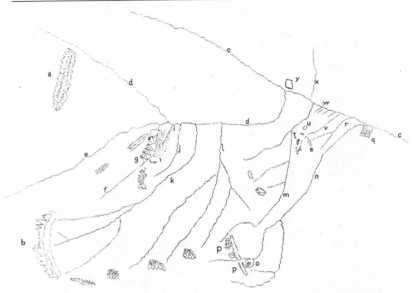

Little Bighorn battlefield and adjacent territory, embracing part of Montana and the Dakotas, drawn at Cheyenne River agency, South Dakota, in 1881. The map as now presented is reduced to one-sixteenth from the original, which is drawn in colors on a sheet of manila paper. The letters were not on the original and are inserted only for reference from the descriptive text, as follows:

a. Wind River mountains, called by the Sioux "the Enemies' mountains."

b. Bighorn mountains.

c. Missouri river.

d. Yellowstone river.

e. Bighorn river.

f. Little Bighorn river, called by the Sioux Greasy Grass creek and Grass Greasy creek.

g. Indian camp.

h. battlefiield.

i. Dry Creek.

j. Rosebud river.

k. Tongue river.

l. Powder river.

m, Little Missouri river.

n, Cheyenne river, called by the Sioux Good river. The North and South forks are drawn but not lettered.

o. Bear butte.

p. Black hills.

q. Cheyenne agency.

r. Moreau or Owl Creek.

s. Thin butte.

t. Rainy butte.

u. White butte.

v. Grand or Ree river.

w. Ree village.

x. White Earth river.

y. Fort Buford.

The Brave Bear and Long Sioux Statement

Editorial note: The Brave Bear and Long Sioux statement is contained in a letter written by George Bent to George Hyde. This letter, partially dated September 1905, is housed in the Bent Collection, Colorado Historical Society. It is reproduced hereafter with their permission.

Long Sioux, also known as Tall Sioux, was a Lakota who had married a woman from Southern Cheyenne tribe. He was a member of the Elk Scrapers of the Cheyenne Dog Soldier Band and a survivor of the battle of Summit Springs in 1869. Tall Sioux later joined the Northern Cheyennes. For information on Brave Bear, see the narrative printed hereafter. The statement which follows is a segment of a much longer letter containing non-relevant matter.

Colony, Oklahoma
September 1905

Brave Bear and Long Sioux tell me [that the] Sioux and Cheyennes were dancing all night after the Custer fight.[1]

---

[1]However, other informants deny that any dances were held on June 25 because of deference shown to bereaved families who were lamenting lost relatives slain in the fight. Nonetheless, weary survivors on Reno Hill distinctly heard the sound of drums beaten monotonously during the long hours of the night.

The big village did not move until they [had] seen troops coming up the Little Big Horn.

[A] good many squaws and children ran to the hills when Custer first came in sight, but all came back and went to where Custer and his men were killed. Brave Bear and Long Sioux say there was lots of fussing and quarreling among [the] Sioux after the fight over horses and guns that were captured. [The] Sioux very often quarrel over the plunder. I have seen this myself.

The Brave Bear Narrative

Editorial note: The Brave Bear narrative is recorded in a letter from George Bent to George Hyde, dated March 8, 1906, and is housed as MSS SC 860 among the special collections of Brigham Young University. It is reproduced hereafter with their permission.

Brave Bear was a Southern Cheyenne and a member of the Dog Soldier Band. He was the owner of a powerful, painted shield and painted lodge. After the defeat of the Dog Soldiers at Summit Springs in 1869, Brave Bear went north and settled with the Northern Cheyenne tribe, marrying one of their women. He was present when the attack on Dull Knife's village took place in 1876, losing a son to a trooper's bullet. Later in life Brave Bear was elected to the civil office of Old Man Chief and became a member of the Council of Forty-Four. The narrative letter which follows was written by George Bent, an educated mixed blood married to a woman of the Southern Cheyennes. The letter was addressed to George Hyde who was a respected anthropologist/historian of the Plains Indian tribes.

Colony, Oklahoma
March 8, 1906

BRAVE BEAR'S STORY OF CUSTER'S FIGHT ON LITTLE BIG HORN

Lots of war parties of Cheyennes and Sioux had just come into the villages from different points [after] making raids. I was with a party that had just returned with lots of plunder. War societies all through the villages were having scalp dances all night.[1] I was about in [the] center of the big village, dancing until daylight when I went to my father's lodge to take sleep as I had been up all night dancing. I had been sleeping for some time when my father woke me up and told me to get up. Fighting was going on [at the] upper village. He told me he had my war horse and shield all ready. As I got up I heard lots of firing.

I took my small sack that had my porcupine-tail hairbrush and my paints. I had to put on [the] same paint that my shield was painted with, and had [to] put it on just as my shield was painted. This was on my face. My father took off my shield [the] blacktail deer tail. This was to [be] tied to my scalp lock. This charm was to turn bullets [away] from me. My father touched my head four times with this tail before tying it on to my scalp lock. This shield my father gave me of course knew all the medicine that belong[ed] to it.[2]

---

[1]In addition to military dances, there were also many social dances held in the village. These latter affairs were particularly liked by the younger people because it afforded them an opportunity to meet single girls.

[2]Among the Cheyennes most shields were believed to possess strong spiritual power, obtained from certain animals which the Cheyennes regarded as having superhuman qualities. These shields were principally divided into two categories: dream shields, owned by individuals, and group shields, which were owned by a band, or a division. The fashion and painting of both types of shields came to an individual in a dream, and no one but the owner was allowed to handle such a shield for fear of violating the taboos connecting with the ownership. It was said that a young man who failed to perform the ceremonies appropriate to the shield would be wounded severely during the battle in which he carried the shield.

As I went out [the] front [of] the lodge to mount my horse, women and children ran by me, saying soldiers were in camp fighting. I heard firing plainly now. My father held my shield towards the sun and said to the shield [and] to the sun to protect me from the bullets. Then he put the shield on my right side and told me to go and die in the battle.

As I started towards the battleground I met lots [of] women and children, mostly Sioux. They told us to hurry up as several of us had now got together and [a] lot more warriors were coming behind us. We were all singing our different society songs, some singing death songs, as this is the custom among all the Indians in going into battles. They also sing these songs when they are attacked and [are] in tight places. I heard lots of this singing at Sand Creek when Chivington attacked the village.[3]

Brave Bear says when he and his crowd got to the battleground, the soldiers were fighting on foot and had their horses in the timber in rear of them. I ran, he says, very close to the soldiers. They were firing in every direction as the Indians were getting around them back at the other end of the firing line of the soldiers.

Two Crow scouts of Custer came charging towards me. I also charged on them. When I got near them they both jumped off their horses and got on [the] side of their horses so they could shoot better. Just then [a] lot of warriors rushed up to count "coe" [coup] on them, but I was first to count

---

[3]On November 29, 1864, units from the New Mexico Infantry and the First and Third Colorado Cavalry attacked a camp of Southern Cheyennes and Arapahos on Sand Creek in present Colorado. This unprovoked attack was directed against an unsuspecting community that had been promised protection by government officials, and which, on the faith of that protection, placed itself in the hands of the troops. This decision proved to be disastrous. During the ensuing massacre, officers and soldiers alike committed untold atrocities on the bodies of women and children. The dead toll amounted to 150 Indians, of which more than one hundred were scalped by soldiers who displayed the trophies during a parade in Denver.

"coe" on one. This gave me [a] big honor or big name by counting first "coe" in [the] Custer battle.[4]

When I looked around towards the soldiers they were running to their horses, [and] Indians were thick as ants behind them. By this time the soldiers made quick for [the] Little Big Horn. The worst of it was [that] the soldiers struck very high banks of the river and all went over. When they struck the water it sounded like [a] cannon going off. This was awful as the bank was awful high.

When I rode to the bank the Indians were shooting the soldiers as they came up out of [the] water. I could see lots of blood in [the] water. I [had] only seen seven soldiers crawl out on the other side of [the] Little Big Horn.[5] The Indians on that side killed them in [a] little while as they had nothing to shoot with [because] they had lost their arms in [the] water.

When I got across the river I saw three companies [of Custer's battalion] making [a] stand and [noticed] one company [on] the other side of them on [a] knoll.[6] I can not understand why the three companies did not try and help

---

[4]The names of these two Crows were Half Yellow Face and White Swan. They were instructed by their interpreter, Mitch Bouyer, to ascend Reno Hill for a reconnaissance, but they instead joined the Ree scouts and rode with Reno's troops into the Little Bighorn valley. Half Yellow Face, known as Big Belly to the Rees, was the Pipe Bearer (leader) of the six Crow scouts attached to Custer's regiment. His tribesman, White Swan (1851–1904), was severely wounded in the right wrist, the thigh, and the shoulder during the engagement in the valley, and was later evacuated on the *Far West*.

According to Brave Bear, both Crows were "couped" on the *west* side of the river, when Reno's skirmish line was still deployed. However, it is possible that Brave Bear may have erred in the location of the incident. According to the Ree, Young Hawk, the wounding of White Swan took place outside a thick grove of trees on the *east* bank of the river, where the victim was found laying on his back, moaning from pain.

[5]A similar impression was held by the Oglala, Red Feather, who stated that only ten of Reno's soldiers reached Reno Hill, while others recalled as few as only four. Brave Bear's statement suggests that many more soldiers may have been killed in the river than first was assumed. In this connection it should be noted that on June 28 a burial party found seven bodies on a shallow sandbar in a bend of the river, a short distance downstream from the retreat crossing.

[6]The sequence in the narrative makes it clear that this was Custer's battalion and not Benteen's. Brave Bear probably saw the deployment on Calhoun Ridge and Custer Hill.

those that jumped off the bank, or why all of them didn't cross over and fight in the village. I think Custer saw he was caught in [a] bad place and would like to have gotten out of it if he could, but he was hemmed in all around and could do nothing [but] only to die then.

These three companies turned all their horses loose; that is, the horses that were not shot down [already].[7] Only one officer stayed on his horse. It did not take long to kill them here. I saw Yellow Nose with a flag coming out [from] among the dead soldiers.[8] Eight soldiers started towards [the] company on [the] knoll. The officer on horse[back] was behind them. [A] Cheyenne charged this officer, [and] this officer shot him in [the] head. [A] Sioux with scalp lock charged at him also, and he shot this Sioux in the breast. Another Indian [then] rode up and shot this officer off his horse. I captured his horse. It was [a] sorrel horse. This officer killed these two Indians. I have been told since [then that] Custer was with that one company on [the] knoll.[9]

---

[7]According to the Two Kettle Lakota, Runs the Enemy, Indians fired upon these troops from the rear (north) side, frightening the led horses which broke away from the holders. Some of these horses rushed upon the ridge where many were shot by Indians firing from the south side, believing the soldiers were charging. This action took place on Calhoun Ridge because it was here that officers of the Montana Column observed the bodies of men and horses thickly strewn about. According to Joe Blummer, a local store owner, these horse bones could still be seen as late as 1904.

[8]This flag was captured on Calhoun Ridge. According to Yellow Nose, a soldier who carried a guidon rode toward him, holding the staff poised like a spear. At the lower end of this staff was a brass ferrule which Yellow Nose in his excitement mistook for a gun. He wrested the guidon away from this soldier and counted coup on him at the same time.

After capturing the flag, Yellow Nose charged the soldiers on the hill a second time. This time, however, he was not so lucky because the remaining soldiers singled him out as a target. A ledger drawing by the Cheyenne, Spotted Wolf, shows Yellow Nose's pony being shot down under a hail of bullets while its rider still carried his lance and the captured guidon. This incident was also remembered by the Oglala, Eagle Elk, who stated that Yellow Nose was shot through the heels and that his pony stumbled, breaking both its legs. Yellow Nose survived this ordeal and later gave this guidon to a bereaved Cheyenne woman who had lost a relative at the hands of the whites.

[9]This officer came from Calhoun Hill, and since he was killed some distance south of Custer Hill, he could not have been General Custer, as Brave Bear first had inferred. The identity of this officer is not known; in fact, we do not even (continued on next page)

I think Custer would have been better off if he had got in among the villages and made his stand there among them and got killed there with his men. I understand [the] whites don't like [to] hear that Custer did not act brave in this battle, but Indians here all think he acted cowardly. Twenty-eight Indians were killed in this battle.

---

know if this man was an officer at all, although his display of conduct reminds us of one. The fact that he rode a sorrel horse suggests that he was a member of C Company, and as a rule the officers rode government horses of the same color as the company to which they were assigned.

If this soldier was indeed an officer of C Company, it could only have been Second Lt. Henry M. Harrington because the company's captain, Tom Custer, was assigned to Headquarters' Staff as Aide-de-Camp to his brother. Harrington rode a large and powerful horse, described as being very fast. Harrington's remains were not identified on the battlefield, and he was declared MIA, and presumed killed.

The Cheyenne slain by this officer was either Black Bear or Limber Bones, the only Cheyennes killed on the east side of Custer Ridge. The identity of the Sioux is not known.

The Thunder Bear Narrative

Editorial note: The Thunder Bear narrative is housed in the Edward Curtis Papers and is listed as "Thunder Bear's Version of Custer's Fight," General Collection #1143, Box 3, Folder 3.8, Natural History Museum of Los Angeles County, California. It is reproduced hereafter with their permission.

A subject search failed to disclose any information on this Yanktonai eyewitness. Edward S. Curtis is chiefly known for his photographs and ethnological notes on the Indians west of the Mississippi. His extensive field work to record the customs and legends of these Indians resulted in his acclaimed *The North American Indian*, which consisted of twenty volumes. The interview which follows was probably conducted in 1907 when Curtis visited the Sioux reservations in the Dakotas. The text has been divided into paragraphs.

[Sioux Reservation, 1907]

The Yanktonai were camping at Old Fort Peck in 1876. Four of us decided to visit Sitting Bull's camp on Pezhi sda wak-pa,[1] Grease Grass river (Little Big Horn). So I, Medi-

---

[1] *Peji Sda Wakpa* 'lush grass river' is a Dakota word. The Lakotas, or *Titonwan*, pronounced it *Peji Sla Wakpa*.

cine Cloud, Iron Bear, and Long Tree, with Medicine Cloud's wife, started in the first part of June. (More likely the latter part of May.) We struck Powder river below where Miles City is now and followed the trail leading southwest.

We had been in the big camp about twenty sleeps when one morning the women who had been gathering turnips came riding in all out of breath and reported that the soldiers were coming. The country, they said, looked as if filled with smoke, so much dust was there. There were four big circles of Sioux and one of Cheyennes in the camp.

The soldiers [of Reno's battalion] charged right up to the edge of the camp, dismounted, and began fighting. The horses became wild and we were still trying to catch them. Very few of us fell. But soon we gathered and charged. It was like a cloud of mosquitos. We rode right up to the soldiers' skirmish line. Indians and horses fell everywhere, some right among the soldiers. But more [Indians] were there and finally we made them run. Then right among them we rode, shooting them down as in a buffalo drive.

They [Custer's battalion][2] ran to the top of a knoll and dismounted, one man holding four horses. We dismounted, too, and filled the gullies that the running water had made in the side of the hill. From there we could shoot straight up at the soldiers. Many of them fell, but the others kept shooting and killing some of us. The fighting continued, and what horses had not been killed, stampeded and rushed down the hill across the river, where the women and children were. The women captured them.

---

[2]There is an apparent break in the sequence of the narrated events. It is at such occasions that Indian accounts appear to be bewildering to students of the battle, bringing into sharp focus the cultural difference of the Indian frame of mind. When reading the Indian accounts, one should be aware that these recollections are nearly always personal recountings of incidents, and that they are rarely meant to present an overall view. Thus, the narrator's statements are based on a series of impressions which convey only that which came under his personal observation. In addition, these statements, more often than not, lack any reference to place and time.

All the time we kept closing in on them. One crowd of the soldiers left the hill and ran down into a deep ravine, but we gathered on the edge and shot them.[3] Pahinhanska [*Pehin Hanska* 'Long Hair,' meaning Gen. Custer] was killed in the middle of his men. We all knew him. His long hair had been cut off. We did not cut him up, or even scalp him.

After the fight was over and we returned to camp, I heard a bugle and saw on a hill three troops of cavalry, one with blacks, one with bays, [and] one with white horses. They were a lot of our young fellows, dressed up in the uniforms of the soldiers and mounted on their horses.[4] After this the young men made ready to charge Reno's men, but just then scouts came from down the river, reporting that a big lot of soldiers were coming.

The Cheyennes, being at the other end of [the] camp, got their horses first and did most of the fighting that occurred near the camp and in the retreat. A black man half-breed[5] and Bloody Knife,[6] the chief scout of the Arikara, were the first ones killed.[7] At the end [of Custer's fight] we rushed among the men on the hill and killed them with clubs and

---

[3]This statement may have reference to Deep Ravine where twenty-eight soldiers were slain during the final phase of the battle.

[4]White horses were ridden by trumpeters; grey horses were assigned to E Company; bays were assigned to F, I, and L Company; and black horses were assigned to D Company. Inasmuch that D Company was assigned to Benteen's battalion, none of its horses could have been captured by the Indians. Yet, a similar statement about black horses present on Custer's battlefield was made by the Cheyenne, Two Moons, who saw these horses at the location where I Company was slain.

[5]This was Isaiah Dorman, a Negro interpreter, who was employed at Fort Rice. In the early 1870s Dorman had operated a woodyard just north of Ft. Yates where he and his Hunkpapa wife lived in a dugout. Dorman accompanied the Seventh Cavalry as a civilian interpreter for Custer's five enlisted Sioux scouts. During Reno's retreat from the valley, Dorman was recognized by the Hunkpapas after killing one of them at close range. Known to the Lakotas as Teats, they riddled his horse with bullets which sealed the rider's fate. Dorman was shot to death by the Hunkpapa, Eagle Robe Woman, in revenge for the slaying of a relative.

[6]Hired as a guide for the expedition, Bloody Knife was a Ree Indian who was killed in the timber, next to Reno. Being part Hunkpapa, he was decapitated and his head stuck on a pole which the Hunkpapas triumphantly displayed in the village.

[7]That unfortunate distinction belongs to Sgt. Miles F. O'Hara of M Company. He was severely wounded on the first skirmish line and was abandoned by the soldiers of his company who ignored his please not to be left behind.

arrows. Even the women, some of them, were there.[8] There was such confusion that no honors could be counted, but we took some scalps from those whose hair was long enough. The Cheyennes got most of them.

Chagha, Ice, a medicine man, was chief of the Cheyennes.[9] Sitting Bull, Tatanka Iyotanka, was chief of the Sioux. His chiefs were Shunka Hanska, Long Dog;[10] I-to-ma-gho-zhi, Rain in the Face;[11] Pizi, Gall;[12] Mato Washte, Pretty Bear;[13] Wi Sapa, Black Moon;[14] Don't Paint His Face; Wanaghi Ska, White Ghost; Tatanka He Geleshka, Spotted Horn

---

[8]One of these women was the Hunkpapa, Moving Robe Woman, who avenged the death of her brother by slaying two of Custer's wounded troopers—shooting one, and hacking the other man to death with a sheath knife.

[9]*Caga* 'Ice,' also known as Ice Bear or Polar Bear, was the Lakota name for White Bull, a renowned shaman of the Northern Cheyennes. He was neither a council chief nor a head soldier, but was treated with the same respect accorded to such men.

[10]*Shunka Hanska* 'Long Dog' or 'Tall Dog,' was a Hunkpapa band leader and the owner of a sacred object which made him bulletproof.

[11]*Ito Magazu* 'Rain in the Face' (1836–1905) was a Hunkpapa who was arrested in 1875 by Capt. Tom Custer for the killing of two civilians. He escaped from Fort Lincoln early in 1876, swearing vengeance on his captor. There are conflicting reports whether Rain actually participated in the Custer battle; however, the extreme mutilation of Tom Custer's body gave rise to immediate speculation about Rain's involvement. His reputation as Tom Custer's slayer was firmly cemented by the writings of Elizabeth Custer and Longfellow's poem, "The revenge of Rain in the Face."

[12]*Pizi* 'Gall' (1840–1893) was a Hunkpapa band leader who was bayonetted by soldiers while resisting arrest in 1867. Gall miraculously survived his ordeal and escaped, and out of vengeance he killed seven whites, among whom was Lt. Eben Cross in 1871. During Reno's attack, Gall's two wives and three children were slain. After his short exile in Canada, Gall surrendered his band to the military at Poplar Creek, Montana, in January 1880. His conduct on the reservation was exemplary, and he later became a justice of the Indian Police Court at Standing Rock. Gall was described as a haughty man who held himself aloof from other people. It was said that his character was stronger than that of Sitting Bull, but that his personality was not as pleasant.

[13]*Mato Waste* 'Pretty Bear,' or rather 'Good Bear,' was the leader of a small Hunkpapa band. He may have been the father of the young Hunkpapa of like name who was wounded in front of Reno's skirmish line, and who was rescued by One Bull, the brother of the Minneconjou, White Bull.

[14]*Wi Sapa* 'Black Moon,' also known as Old Black Moon, was an uncle of Sitting Bull and Gall, and was the leader of a Hunkpapa band. He was described as a loquacious man who was fond of joking. After his exile in Canada, he surrendered to the military in 1881 and died on the Standing Rock Reservation in 1888. His son was Young Black Moon, a head soldier who had charge of the Hunkpapa camp police at the Little Bighorn. He was slain in front of Reno's skirmish line.

Bull;[15] Tashunka Witko, Crazy Horse, [and] Wopide, Medicine Bag That Burns.[16]

This last man's [Wopide] two brothers were killed on the hilltop, and his sisters came with axes and knocked the brains out of some wounded soldiers.[17] One soldier got down to the river and lay there on his back in the water with only his nose showing. Some Indians watched him for a while and one shot him with a six-shooter. Sitting Bull was not in the fighting. He walked up and down, talking to the warriors.

After the fight the Indian soldiers said nobody was to leave camp, for there were many from other agencies and they did not want the fight reported.[18] But Iron Bear and I got away in the night and came back to Fort Peck. Rain in the Face was the bravest man there.

Nineteen Sioux and seventeen Cheyennes were killed;[19] but a great many were wounded. Seven Sioux and two Cheyennes were killed by Reno's men.[20] Many horses were killed. Many soldiers shot wild into the air. That is why we

---

[15]*Tatanka He Gleska* 'Spotted Horn Bull,' was a Hunkpapa warrior and a member of Sitting Bull's body guard. He was killed with Sitting Bull during the latter's arrest on December 15, 1890. Spotted Horn Bull's wife was Pretty White Buffalo Woman who was known among the Lakotas for her eloquence.

[16]*Wopide* 'Medicine Bag that Burns,' or, actually, 'Burns the Medicine Bag,' was the nickname given to the Hunkpapa, Crow King, who, in a fit of anger, burned the medicine bundle of a shaman who failed to save the life of his brother Tall Bear who had tuberculosis.

[17]The names of Crow King's two brothers were Swift Bear and White Bull, who were both killed on Reno's battlefield during the soldiers' retreat. Other sources confirm reports of mutilations by squaws roaming Custer's battlefield, notably on Custer Hill where Tom Custer's remains were horribly mangled by enraged Sioux women. Significantly, a burial party on June 28 reported finding an axe just below Custer Hill, the dried blood on the edged head leaving little to the imagination.

[18]Thunder Bear's statement is borne out by Kill Eagle, a Blackfoot Lakota agency Indian, who was detained with his band by Hunkpapa camp police. Kill Eagle reported that the police burned several of his lodges, killed ten of his ponies, and assaulted a number of his men.

[19]Although the total casualty count of thirty-six is quite accurate, only seven Cheyennes lost their lives: Roman Nose, Limber Bones, Noisy Walking, Cut Belly, Whirlwind, Black Bear aka Crippled Hand, and Lame White Man aka Black Body.

[20]The Indian casualty count incurred as a result of Reno's attack amounted to twenty-one people.

think they were drunk. If they had not been they would have killed more of us. There were more than 2000 tipis in the camp, and in every one three or four young men, besides the older men.

(The news was brought to Fort Peck by Thunder Bear and Iron Bear. They were ferried across the river by the interpreter, Joe Culbertson, a Blackfeet half breed, then a scout, who at once rode to Fort Bufort, where another scout had already gotten in with the news.)

The first charge on the camp was about noon and lasted less than two hours.

The Charles Corn Letters

Editorial note: The Charles Corn letters are housed in the Walter M. Camp Collection, Little Bighorn Battlefield National Monument, Montana, and are reproduce hereafter with their permission.

Charles Corn was an educated Lakota who was born about 1853. He was the son of Frank Corn, an Oglala full-blood. The letters were addressed to William O. Taylor, a former soldier of Company A, Seventh Cavalry, who had fought in the battle of the Little Bighorn. Taylor had submitted these letters to Walter M. Camp for his evaluation. Camp was an avocational historian of the Plains Indian wars. The text which follows has been corrected as to spelling errors.

Thunder Butte, South Dakota
September 15, 1909

William O. Taylor.

Dear Sir:

I have received your letter and will now answer you. You first asked me if the Indians knew you (the soldiers) were coming. No, we did not know anything until you fired on us.

Second question: How many Indians were killed[?] There were three battles. [In] the first fight 4 Indians were killed. The second fight 21 Indians were killed. The third fight, where you were up on the hill, 2 Indians were killed. So, all together 27 Indians were killed.

Third question: Did the Indians know that it was Custer[?] No, we did not know it was Custer until quite awhile afterwards.

Fourth question: How long did the battle last[?] It lasted about two hours.

The last question. There was one man [who] killed himself about a mile from the others. He was riding a dark bay horse and was very fast, but he killed himself.[1] He shot himself through the head. He could have lived because he was riding a fast horse. After the battle I saw a dark sorrel with white on his legs and I heard it was Custer's horse. The horse was owned by a Santee named Red End.[2]

There were five tribes of us, but the soldiers wanted to kill us so we had to fight for our lives. You tried to get our children and wives, so I was willing to die fighting for them that day. That battle is still fresh in my mind. The children and the women were crying so we tried to defend ourselves. Well, friend, lets shake hands as we are now friends. I was 23 years old then and was not afraid of anything. I shall be glad to hear from you again.

I am your friend,
Charlie Corn
Thunder Butte
S.D.

---

[1]As a result of an excess in bay horses, this color was distributed to three units of Custer's battalion: Companies F, I, and L.

[2]Red End, or Red Top, is a translation deviant of Bloody Antler Tips, whose son, Noisy Walking, was said to have captured Custer's horse.

Thunder Butte, S.D.
April 23, 1910

Mr. W. O. Taylor
        Orange
                N.J.
    Dear Sir:
        Your letter of recent date received some time ago and
was glad to hear from you as usual. I am [a] little slow in
answering in regards to . . . all the questions you ask about the
Custer War.
        . . . About half an hour [after Reno's attack] the big fight
came off and I was the first fellow [to] kill one of the Custer
soldiers. While they were fighting, the women folks move on
the other side of the Little Big Horn and the soldiers were on
other side. Some of them went around one way and the others
[stayed] on one side. They [are] not very many on the west side
and I was on the west side. All at once the Indians started for
the soldiers. Then the soldiers were split up and some of them
headed for a creek. Before they got to the creek [there was]
nothing left but one, and this soldier were run down the creek
and some of the Indians were chasing. Before the Indians got
to this one soldier he shot himself right through the jaw,[3] and
then the Custer War won't last very long, and I like to know
how many soldiers were kill[ed] that time in three wars that
time, and I tho[ught] I was [a] dead person at the end of the
war. I wasn't kill[ed] and I was twenty-three years old at that
time. Now I am fifty-seven years old and I did not think I live
that long. Well friend I . . . close with best regards to you.
        Your truly friend
            Mr. Chas Corn

---

[3] Although the evidence is at variance, Walter Camp concluded that this individual
was probably Cpl. John Foley of C Company, whose body was found on a little rise
just north of Medicine Tail Coulee, some 400 yards east of the river.

The Yellow Nose Interview

Editorial note: The Yellow Nose narrative is contained in a newspaper dispatch printed in the (Chicago) *Inter Ocean,* issue of March 24, 1912, of which a clipping is housed in the author's collection.

Born about 1854, Yellow Nose was a Ute Indian who was captured with his mother near the Rio Grande in 1858 by a Cheyenne war party under Lean Bear. This prominent Cheyenne adopted Yellow Nose as his son, and although he took the boy's mother as his wife, this woman twice attempted to escape and finally succeeded in 1860. Ironically, a few years after her return to the Utes, her daughter, a younger sister of Yellow Nose, was also captured by the Cheyennes. Yellow Nose grew up to become one of the most renowned warriors among the Cheyennes. At age eleven, he received a severe gunshot wound in the chest during one of the many skirmishes with the whites in the Platte Valley. Although he was a member of Tall Bull's Dog Soldier Band, he survived the destruction of their village at Summit Springs in 1869, and joined the Northern Cheyennes. After their surrender, Yellow Nose settled in Oklahoma Territory and in later years became a respected shaman.

[Geary, Oklahoma, 1911]

YELLOW NOSE SAID TO BE THE INDIAN WHO KILLED CUSTER

... The belief [is] firmly held among the old warriors of the Northern Cheyenne and Arapahoe tribes in Oklahoma that Custer was slain by Yellow Nose, a Ute Indian now living on his allotment on the North Canadian River, near the town of Geary, Ok. The Indians have believed this for thirty-five years. Yellow Nose, who is not a boaster, merely says that he killed a man, an officer, who, other Indians said, was Custer. Yellow Nose had not seen Custer prior to the battle.

This man, whose tribesmen so resolutely state he took Custer's life, is now about 57 years old and well preserved, save that he has been blind for many years from a blow across the forehead in the Little Big Horn fight, which eventually destroyed his eyesight. His body is scarred with many wounds received in battle. He will open his shirt and point to a hardened spot on his chest where a bullet tore through him when McKenzie's [sic] men gave battle in Powder River canyon.[1] Yellow Nose was peering over an embankment, not suspecting that any danger was near at hand, when he was shot from ambush.

When Yellow Nose was 4 years old he was captured from his people by the Northern Cheyennes, one of whose women he married. He was a scout under General Lawton at Fort Robinson and later was given similar employment at Fort Reno. On the plains country he met the French-Cheyenne

---

[1]On November 26, 1876, units of the Fourth and Fifth Cavalry under Col. Ranald S. MacKenzie surprised and destroyed a Cheyenne village of 120 lodges of which Dull Knife and Wild Hog were the principal chiefs. It was learned later from the Cheyennes that this disaster was brought about by the obstinacy and arrogance of Last Bull, head soldier of the Fox Soldier Society. In this battle, Yellow Nose, who wore a magnificent warbonnet, sustained a gunshot to the right side of the chest, but he nonetheless continued to fight the soldiers.

scout, Edward [*sic*] Guerrier,[2] and their friendship brought Yellow Nose to Oklahoma in the early 70s. There was a constant passing to and from of the Northern and Southern Indians in those days.

Yellow Nose tells a circumstantial story which old warriors in Oklahoma support with their own testimony and evidence that he was the man who killed Custer. A number of Southern Cheyennes from Oklahoma were visiting the Northern Cheyennes at the time of the battle and took part in the engagement. They brought numerous relics from the battlefields to Oklahoma. In the neighborhood of Cantonment, Ok., may still be found guns taken from the dead troopers of the Seventh Cavalry. For a number of years George Bent,[3] a mixed-blood Cheyenne who lives at Colony, Ok., owned Custer's pocket compass[4] given to him by Bull Head, a

---

[2]Edmond G. Guerrier (1840–1921) was the son of William Guerrier, a French trader, and a Southern Cheyenne woman. After his father's death in 1851, he attended school in St. Louis, but discontinued his education after a while and returned to his mother's people. Edmond Guerrier served as an interpreter for Gen. Custer in 1867, and worked as a scout for the Fifth Cavalry in late 1868 and 1869. He was later employed by the trading firm of Lee & Reynolds, and in 1875 married Julia Bent, the daughter of William Bent and Yellow Woman. The town of Geary, Oklahoma, is named after him.

[3]George Bent (1843–1918) was the son of William Bent, a well-known trader, and Owl Woman, the daughter of the Sacred Arrow Keeper of the Southern Cheyennes. George Bent received a college education in St. Louis, and upon graduation joined the cavalry branch of the Confederate Army. After his capture by Union soldiers in 1862, he was released in the care of his father, and settled with his mother's people. He was wounded during the Sand Creek massacre in 1864, and joined the Cheyenne Dog Soldiers in their retaliatory raids against white soldiers and civilians. After the surrender of the Cheyennes, Bent settled down on the reservation in Oklahoma and served as an interpreter and counselor for many Cheyennes who looked to him for guidance and protection. Although his life was marred by broken marriages, alcoholism, and corrupt business dealings, in later years George Bent felt a need to reflect on it, and that of the Cheyennes, by writing hundreds of letters and granting countless interviews.

[4]Bent was told by Bull Head that he had removed this compass from General Custer's pocket on Custer Hill. However, Lt. Oscar Long learned from Cheyenne Indian Scouts that a compass, along with a pair of field glasses, was taken from an officer killed on Calhoun Hill. The needle of this compass was protected by a wooden box, rather than by cardboard as was common at that time.

Southern Cheyenne.[5] Bent sold the compass in 1879 to George Reynolds of the Indian trading firm of Lee & Reynolds, then at Camp Supply, Ok. As the story runs among the Oklahoma Indians, Custer and his men were first decoyed to the locality broken by ravines by Long Sioux and a companion. Long Sioux lives near Cantonment.

When the grass began greening on the plains in the spring of 1876, Yellow Nose started with his wife to visit her relatives in the North. Throughout the Sioux and Northern Cheyenne country there was great unrest among the Indians, and it was apparent that war was at hand. Yellow Nose lingered until it was unsafe for him to attempt to journey home, as small bands of Indians were in as great danger of losing their lives as were white men, if caught traveling through the country. About the middle of June war parties began bringing in reports of the presence of troops in the Tongue River country, and Yellow Nose went several times with scout parties to observe the soldiers. Finally the Indians gave battle on the Rosebud,[6] and then retired in the direction of the Little Big Horn, Yellow Nose moving with them.

A report spread among the Indians that troops were advancing with Shoshone scouts, and inasmuch that General Crook had retired to the southward, the Indians expected the advance from that direction. To their utter surprise the troops came from the east under the command of Custer. There was much bitterness against Custer among the Indians because of his alleged massacre of the Black Kettle village

---

[5]Bull Head was a Southern Cheyenne council chief of the Dog Soldier Band and a survivor of the Summit Springs battle. He had a good combat reputation and was the owner of a special medicine which cured snake bites and healed gunshot wounds.

[6]The Battle of the Rosebud took place on June 17, 1876, when a united force of Sioux and Cheyenne warriors fought a victory over units of the Second and Third Cavalry and Fourth and Ninth Infantry, the whole commanded by General George Crook.

of Southern Cheyennes, on the Washita River, in Indian Territory, now Oklahoma.[7]

The village of the different tribes stretched for several miles along the west bank of the Little Big Horn. Yellow Nose went from village to village on the night of June 24 to see the dancing. Strict orders had been given by the war chiefs forbidding the firing of guns in camp, as the near approach of the troops was to be made known by two mounted warriors, who were to ride at full speed and fire two shots as they passed each village.

The battle was on Sunday, a warm, bright day. Farthest down the river was the camp of the Northern Cheyennes, where stood the lodge of the great war chief Crazy Horse. About noon, Crazy Horse, Yellow Nose and other Indians were in the river bathing when the firing of guns was heard up the river. Reno and his men had crossed the Little Big Horn and were charging the upper villages, only to be beaten back in confusion and under such circumstances as came near dishonoring Reno.

Yellow Nose does not speak nor understand the English language. What he said in recounting his experiences was translated by his friend, Edward Guerrier, the old scout. Here he plunged into the detail of his narrative. Yellow Nose was confident that the Sioux would have destroyed Reno had they [the Sioux] not charged so quickly and eagerly in defense of their women and children, who thereby were given time to scramble onto ponies or flee on foot and escape westward. Had the Sioux held back and let Reno come further down the river they could have surrounded him and cut him off from the hills in which he afterwards found refuge.

---

[7]The Battle of the Washita was fought on November 27, 1868, when the Seventh Cavalry under General Custer destroyed a Cheyenne village of fifty-one lodges. The Indian dead amounted to thirteen males, sixteen women, and nine children, for a total of thirty-eight casualties. Custer's official report listed an inflated count of 103 dead warriors.

Yellow Nose and his companions were delayed in rallying to the alarm, owing to the absence of their ponies, which had been driven away to graze. By the time they got their mounts they discovered another body of troops eastward across the river. The Cheyennes divided, some going to resist Reno while others, including Yellow Nose, crossed the Little Big Horn where a small stream or gulch debouched from the east.[8]

Climbing to a promontory formed by this gulch, the Indians saw troops advancing toward them along the crest of the divide that ran back from the Little Big Horn. Yellow Nose was mounted on a fleet, wiry pony in advance of his companions, whom the soldiers evidently thought were few in numbers, as the crossing was difficult at this point. The mistake of the soldiers became quickly apparent when Indians were seen literally springing from the ground. The galloping cavalrymen pulled down to a trot. The Cheyennes were not so well armed as the Sioux, who carried quantities of ammunition fastened around their waists, chests and arms.

The soldiers fired first from their horses, dismounting only after they saw that the Indians were not intimidated.[9] The regimental band began playing to the astonishment of the Indians, but the musicians threw away their instruments for guns.[10]

The soldiers changed from a stand to a retreat as they were

---

[8]This was probably present Medicine Tail Ford and its streambed, Medicine Tail Coulee, named after the Crow Indian who lived on this allotment.

[9]The deployment took place along Calhoun Ridge, and although Yellow Nose does not mention it, his tribesmen—White Shield, Little Hawk, and Young Two Moon—remember that he made several mounted charges at these soldiers, on the south slope of Calhoun Ridge. After his first charge, a mounted soldier, thought to have been an officer, was shot and fell from his horse. This charge, which Yellow Nose made in company of Contrary Big Belly and Chief Comes in Sight, Cheyennes, frightened the soldiers' horses which tried to break away from their holders. After this charge, Yellow Nose made several more runs, and on his final charge, the fourth, all the Cheyennes followed him and rode through the soldiers on the ridge. It was at this point that Yellow Nose captured a guidon and counted coup with it on a mounted soldier.

[10]The regimental band was left behind at the Powder River Depot. The music heard by the Indian audience came from trumpets blown in unison. The musical notes may have been a rendition of Garry Owen, the Seventh's battle tune.

crowded upon by increasing and overwhelming numbers. Yellow Nose said that they made three stands. It was the purpose of the Indians to get in the rear of the troops and gain the east slope of the ridge. This the soldiers bravely resisted, and in their fury to dislodge the troops the Indians precipitately exposed themselves to a galling fire in the open. It was not until the close of the fight that the soldiers were driven to the west slope of the ridge.

At first the soldiers knelt and took deliberate aim, each fourth man holding the horses. "Some stood up and shot like this," said Yellow Nose, leaning far forward and clutching an imaginary gun. As the confusion, perhaps despair, increased after the retreat from the first stand, each soldier took possession of his own horse, possibly to be better able to escape if the battle went against them.[11]

Yellow Nose declared that this merely hastened the disaster that followed. The held horses grew wild with fright, and their rearing and plunging made it impossible for the soldiers to shoot with steadiness and accuracy, many pulling the trigger while their guns pointed straight above them. Riderless horses stampeded in every direction, leaving their dead behind, and were caught by the Indians and taken across the river.[12]

Yellow Nose had never seen Custer. He twice encountered the man whose body was found after the battle and identified by the Indians as that of Custer. Yellow Nose had shot a trooper, and, in accordance with Indian custom, was running

---

[11]In an interview published in the *Indian School Journal*, issue of November 1905, Yellow Nose explained that the soldiers had hobbled some of their horses by drawing the animals' heads down and tying the reins to their forefeet. Since the Indian charge came so sudden, there was little time to untie the hobbles, and a number of soldiers were killed next to these hobbled horses.

[12]According to Yellow Nose, the bolting horses filled the air with blinding dust which, together with the black smoke of firing, caused great confusion. He added that the yells of the Indians, the rattle of musketry, and the tramp of horses' feet were deafening. In the ensuing turmoil the Indians shot a number of their own warriors by mistake.

forward to strike the body with a stick, which in the Cheyenne language is called "koos." The soldier called for help when he saw his enemy bearing down upon him, and several mounted comrades rushed to his rescue. One of these men fired at Yellow Nose at such close range that his eyes and face are still speckled with the [black] powder. The bullet missed Yellow Nose, wounding his horse in the neck. Yellow Nose was struck a heavy glancing blow across the forehead with the gunsight, blinding him for a moment and filling his eyes with blood.[13]

This same man who had fired at him was next seen by Yellow Nose at a small mound on the ridge and on foot, with about thirty men gathered around him. He was bareheaded and armed only with a pistol. As the Indians bore down upon this group, a number of the soldiers apparently lost courage and ran to lower ground, close to the base of the mound. The officer shouted loudly to the men and drew nearer to them when he found that they did not hear him or were unwilling to obey him.[14]

The appearance of this man was so striking and gallant that Yellow Nose decided that to kill him would be a feat of more than ordinary prowess. Yellow Nose was armed only with an old cavalry saber, having lost his gun. This saber had belonged

---

[13]However, in the *Journal,* Yellow Nose does not mention the glancing blow from the soldier's gun barrel, but recalls that the gash in his forehead was caused by a gunshot, and that the bullet struck his war pony in the head but did not disable it.

[14]This is a reference to Custer Hill where survivors found the bodies of forty-two men. Ten of these corpses lay on a little elevation, some 30 feet in diameter. Gen. George A. Custer was found near the southwestern edge of this elevation, behind a horse, his right leg resting across the body of an unidentified soldier, while his back was slumped against the bodies of Sgt. John Vickory, the regimental color bearer who lay faceup, and Chief Trumpeter Henry Voss, who lay across Vickory's head, Voss laying facedown. Some twenty feet back from the General, toward the eastern perimeter of the elevation, lay the extremely mutilated body of Capt. Tom Custer. Nearby lay Lt. William W. Cooke, his thighs slashed and one of his long, black whiskers scalped. The fourth officer on the crest was Lt. Algernon A. Smith whose body was riddled with arrows. Of the remaining four enlistees, the names of only three are known: Private John Kennedy, of L Company, who lay near Cooke, and Privates John Parker and Edward C. Driscoll, of I Company, who were both found near the eastern ridge of the elevation.

to a boyhood friend, a Shoshone,[15] at whose death his mother had given the saber to Yellow Nose. The battle had gone against the soldiers so heavily at this point that the officer stood finally alone. With saber drawn, Yellow Nose rode headlong at his enemy, prepared to cut him down at a stroke.

Already wounded, and trembling with fright, Yellow Nose's pony bolted when the officer fired at close range with a small pistol, but missed both man and horse. Getting his pony in hand again, Yellow Nose charged a second time, and again the officer fired and the pony sprang aside and beyond him. Determined to get within striking distance, Yellow Nose gathered himself for a third onslaught. As he drew near, the pistol was not fired—it was empty. He came squarely upon the officer, who bent his knees as it to ward off the blow of the uplifted saber. Yellow Nose struck him with terrible violence on the back of the head and the man sunk to the ground in a heap.[16]

---

[15]This Shoshone boy was a captive who was raised by the Cheyennes. Since Yellow Nose was a captive also, the two boys found a common bond which was further strengthened by the racial teasing from Cheyenne boys.

[16]In the *Journal* article Yellow Nose revealed that this man was bareheaded and that his long hair was flowing in the breeze. Yellow Nose added that he did not know General Custer, and made clear that stories told by Indians claiming to have recognized Custer during the fight were mostly lies. He explained that he encountered Custer twice, but that he did not know who Custer was until his body was found after the battle. Yellow Nose recognized the man who he had slain by his buckskin suit, the beads on the fringe, the auburn hair, and the distinguished appearance. This same man was identified by others as General Custer.

Despite these convincing observations, the facts of evidence do not corroborate Yellow Nose's statement. Eyewitnesses who viewed Custer's body stated that only four wounds were found on the corpse, and that two of these were caused by gunshots. One of these wounds was in the head where a bullet had crashed into the left temple, about halfway between the ear and the eye. The second gunshot wound was found in the rib cage, just below the heart. A third wound was observed in Custer's left thigh where a knife slash had opened a deep gash in the flesh and had exposed the bone. The fourth and final wound was in the genitals, which were pierced by an arrow.

Other than the bullet wound in Custer's temple, no other evidence of disfigurement of the cranium has ever come to light. It stands to reason, therefore, that General Custer could not have been the individual who was struck in the head with a saber. However, Yellow Nose's description of the victim's clothing fits Capt. Tom Custer very well, and he apparently was one of the last to die on Custer Hill. Furthermore, his facial features were obliterated by a broken cranium, which was flattened by repeated blows to the back of the head.

The Two Moons Narrative

Editorial note: The Two Moons manuscript was submitted to the author by Frank L. Mercatante in 1993, and is presently housed in the author's collection. Mr. Mercatante is a nationally-known book dealer in Grand Rapids, Michigan, who specializes in rare and out-of-print books on Custer and the Western Frontier. The origin of this manuscript is unknown.

The Northern Cheyenne, Two Moons (1842–1917), was the son of Carries the Otter, an Arikara captive married into the Cheyenne tribe. Two Moons was a minor chief of the Fox Society. After the surrender of the Cheyennes in 1877, he enlisted as an Indian Scout, and as a result of his pleasant personality, his friendliness towards the whites, and his ability of get along with the military, he was selected head chief by Col. Nelson A. Miles. This appointment was later ratified by the Cheyennes. It was said that he had been blind since the early 1900s, but that he had miraculously regained his eyesight during the last few years of his life. For additional interviews with Two Moons, see Hardorff, *Cheyenne Memories of the Custer Fight,* pp. 95–134.

New Capitol Hotel, Washington City
Monday, March 3, 1913

Interview of Chief Two Moons, of Lame Deer, Montana. Henry Leeds, of Lower Brule (Sioux), South Dakota, interpreting.

Two Moons says he and his Cheyennes were in the battle of Tongue River on March 17, 1876.[1] There were 200 Sioux warriors there under Crazy Horse.[2] There were more Cheyennes than Sioux, but he does not remember how many. There were no Indians but Cheyennes and Sioux at the battle of Tongue River.

Battle of the Rosebud, June 17, 1876. There were no Indians but Cheyennes and Sioux in the battle of the Rosebud. Sitting Bull was not at the battle of either Tongue River or the Rosebud.[3] He says they fought Gen. Crook at Rosebud. Three *Cheyennes were killed at Rosebud* [italics in original].[4] He says there must have been between 20 and 30 Indians killed at the battle of the Little Big Horn. There were seven (7) Cheyennes killed.

---

[1]On March 17, 1876, a military strike force under command of Col. Joseph J. Reynolds surprised a Cheyenne winter camp on the Powder River. The Cheyennes, however, rallied under Two Moons and staged a counter attack, forcing Reynolds to abandon the field. After his retreat to the main column, rumors began to circulate that Reynolds had bungled the affair, which led to his court-martial and early retirement the following year.

[2]According to the Oglala Shirt Wearer, He Dog, who was a close friend of Crazy Horse, only ten lodges of Oglalas were present when the Cheyenne camp was attacked. He Dog remembered the details of this incident clearly because he had lost seven prized ponies as a result of this attack.

[3]Sitting Bull did take part in the Rosebud fight, according to his nephews, One Bull and White Bull, who were both with him on the battlefield that day. Sitting Bull, however, did not take a leading part in the battle because of his weakened constitution, having sacrificed one hundred pieces of his flesh during the Sun Dance held on the Rosebud on June 14.

[4]The names of only two Cheyennes are known, namely Black Sun and Scabby. Black Sun, a young man known to the Lakotas as Water Dog, sustained a gunshot to the spine and was buried that night in the rimrocks overlooking the battlefield. Scabby was an older man who was mortally wounded from a gunshot to the abdomen. He died on Prairie Dog Creek about June 20. Some Lakotas later recalled a Cheyenne who had thrown his life away in battle, singing: "I do not wish to be an old man, this day is mine to die." This may have been the third Cheyenne casualty spoken of by Two Moons.

Two Moons told me the first time I met him at the New Capitol Hotel, that when the Indians started to attack Custer, word came to him that the women were leaving the camp and leaving their clothing behind; and that he went back and directed them to remove all such things with them.

At the same time he stated that he and his Cheyennes helped to drive Reno across the river, and when that was done . . . [they] left a guard to keep Reno on the ridge, and then they went back down the river to the attack on Custer.

At another time he told me that it was a Cheyenne woman who discovered the approach of Custer and gave the alarm that the soldiers were coming.

He told me repeatedly that Custer did *not* cross the Little Big Horn.

He said that when the fight was deadliest and the soldiers were surrounded, a man stood upon the ridge waving his sword in view of the several troops which occupied various positions. This was probably Custer himself.[5]

The White Horse Troops[6] fought with signal desperation. If the others had not given up, but had fought with equal stubbornness of the White Horse Troop, Custer would have driven the Indians from the field.

The Indians knocked soldiers from their horses with their tomahawks.

March 4, 1913

Willis T. Rowland, Two Moons['] own Interpreter, [from] Lame Deer, Montana.[7]

---

[5]The only officer to carry a saber on the expedition was Lt. Charles A. DeRudio. According to the latter, Custer never carried a saber on campaigns.

[6]The reference to the White Horse Troops identifies E Company which rode grey horses.

[7]Born along the Platte in 1862, Willis T. Rowland was the son of William Young Rowland, a Kentucky native, and a Southern Cheyenne woman. Willis, who was known as Long Forehead, married the daughter of the respected Cheyenne, Elk River, and served as a Cheyenne interpreter nearly his entire life.

When he [Two Moons] came back from driving Reno across the river to attack Custer, he set the women to removing the goods with them. All at once a man cried out, "Some more soldiers coming! There are more soldiers now than up above."

When he reached the women he told the women to go and pack up and be ready to move.

When Custer came in he marched as though he was going to cross the river at the point above the [present battlefield] reservation. When he got to within a few yards of the Little Horn, shots from the Ind[ian]s on the opposite side turned him, so that his course was thrown about ½ a mile away from the river.

([On] page 9 is a map [which is reproduced below.])

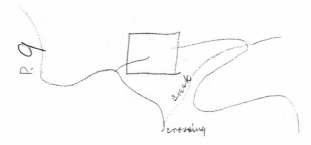

When Custer got on top where the [present kill site] stones are, the troops dismounted and they tried to lead the horses down into a gulch.[8]

The Grey Horse Company was the only troop that held

---

[8]This is probably a reference to Calhoun Ridge, behind which, on the north side, Calhoun Coulee descends, where the led horses may have been sheltered.

their horses. Each man held his own, and not a shot was fired while this was going on. They were making preparations.

After showing the women what to do, Two Moons got back to the battlefield, [and] he rode up and down in front of his men and told them to get ready to charge.

On that creek where Custer came down there were a few Sioux only who had joined the Cheyennes on that north side of the river; they were all Cheyennes except these few Sioux.[9]

After he got his men ready he ordered his men to charge. They charged right up the sloping ground and hill on the soldiers who stood where the first line of [marble] stones is [on Calhoun Ridge].

The soldier fire was so heavy that the Cheyennes had to fall back. He then ordered a second charge, with same result. Immediately he ordered a third charge, which was made. The Indians did not stop this time, but drove the soldiers. This did not last long; it was about all of the fight; after this it was merely a slaughter.[10]

Two Moons now swept to the right and north of the ridge. There was a White Horse [Troop], a Bay Horse Troop, and a Black Horse Troop. The Grey Horse is what he has called the White Horse. The horses in the gulch were now turned loose by the soldiers and they fled toward the river. Some [horses] were caught tied together; some jumped into the

---

[9]According to the Oglala, Eagle Elk, this party consisted of nine warriors, including himself, who were the first ones to charge the soldiers. Among these warriors was a Cheyenne, whose indentity Eagle Elk did not know, who charged ahead of the others, and who captured a guidon from a soldier. This was probably the Cheyenne, Yellow Nose.

[10]The few words of this paragraph accurately describe the Indian view of the Custer Battle, which, for all practical purposes, ended with the fall of Calhoun Hill. Although it has generally been assumed that the soldiers at this location were killed by a sweeping Sioux force under Gall, it now appears that Cheyenne warriors spearheaded the destruction. In fact, some Sioux combatants, among whom He Dog, Oglala tribal historian, later stated that the Cheyennes took the leading part in the fight because the advance of Custer's troops threatened their camp.

river before the Indians got there, but the Ind[ian]s got them all.

He says the fight did not last more than 2 ½ hours from beginning to end.

The young people of the Ind. camp must have robbed the dead of clothing for [the] next day they appeared up the river above the camp mounted on captured horses, dressed in soldier clothing, which led the Ind[ian]s to think other troops were coming, [and] which alarmed the camp until it was discovered who these mounted persons were.

Orders were given to starve Reno out; but after Custer was destroyed Indian scouts were sent below and Terry's soldiers were seen coming, so that [the] next morning the camp packed up and the Indians withdrew.

Wednesday Evening, Feb. [March?] 5, 1913

The Cheyennes crossed the Little Big Horn at the mouth of the creek above the [present battlefield] Reservation. The Sioux crossed at the crossing below the Reservation.[11]

Two Moons says this is the fifth time he had given his account of the Battle of the Big Horn; four times Rowland's father, Wm. Rowland, was the interpreter, and now Willis T. Rowland, the son, is interpreting.

(The next page is a map [which is reproduced at right.])

1.   This circle shows where the dead daughter of a Sioux Chief was place[d] away in a tepee, a day or two before Custer came along; and when he arrived his scouts burned the tepee.[12]

2.   This is where Reno made his stand on the hill.

3.   This is the place, about 3 miles from the Little Horn,

---

[11]Evidence suggests that the Cheyennes crossed the river at Medicine Tail Coulee, while some of the Sioux may have crossed at Deep Ravine, also known as Crazy Horse Gully.

[12]This funeral lodge stood near the lower forks of Reno Creek, some four miles east of the Little Bighorn. Two Moons is mistaken in his identification of the deceased,

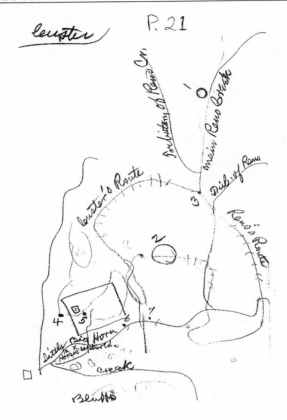

where Custer halted and separated his forces and sent Reno by the route marked above Reno Creek.

4.   A man in buckskin was shot at "4" and he staggered to "5" and fell. The Ind[ian]s have always kept this a secret for fear that the whites would try to punish [them]. It must have been Custer.

---

whose name was Little Wolf, known as the brother of Chief Circling Bear, a leader of a Sans Arc band. Little Wolf died in his lodge from a gunshot wound to the abdomen, sustained in the Rosebud Fight. This funeral lodge was burned by a squad of soldiers from F Company, which advanced in front of Custer's column. According to the Hunkpapa, Has Horns, some of the older Lakotas referred to Reno Creek as Little Wolf Creek in memory of their slain tribesman.

W[illis] T. Rowland, who sat on the field with his uncle, Roan Bear,[13] who was a brother to his mother and spoke good English, (now dead) who was in the battle, says his uncle told him that the Gray Horse Troop stood at the [present] monument with their horses, but finally had to let them go, being surrounded and hard pressed.[14]

Ro[w]land says a Troop was deployed on the ridge where the first fighting took place; another Troop was deployed at right angles, thus:

first line   second troop

The second line advanced north over the ridge and were killed.[15]

When the Custer column was discovered, word was sent up to those pressing Reno, and were told to leave a guard to hold Reno, and to come down and help against Custer. The Sioux crossed at the lower place and waited in the breaks concealed west of the [present] monument. When the Sioux

---

[13]Roan Bear, or Red Bear, was a sub chief of the Kit Fox Society and was one of the first Cheyenne warriors to oppose Custer's force at Medicine Tail Ford. After the surrender in 1876, he and his brothers, Hard Robe and Little Fish, enlisted in the Indian Scouts and served with MacKenzie's troops against Dull Knife's Cheyennes. In 1877 Roan Bear's wife ran off with another man. As settlement Roan Bear asked for a dog meal, which was the value he placed on this unfaithful woman. This passive expression of contempt, the restraint of temper, and the display of dignity were behavior traits common among Cheyenne leaders.

[14]This observation took place near the end of the battle and is confirmed by the Minneconjou, Iron Hawk, and others. Some mistook the stampeding grey horses for a mounted charge by the soldiers.

[15]This statement has reference to the junction of Calhoun Ridge and Custer Ridge where units from Keogh's battalion were deployed along the slopes. A similar statement was made by enlisted Indian Scouts who accompanied Lt. Pope and other officers to the Little Bighorn in 1877. According to these scouts, the soldiers at this location fought a valiant fight and caused the deaths of nearly all the Indian casualties sustained on Custer's battlefield.

began firing, the Cheyennes swung around north of the ridge to avoid Sioux bullets.[16]

The Sioux conquerors found so much whiskey on the horses that many of them got full.[17]

On the map made by Rowland at "6" and "7" were the two Cheyenne guards posted, and No. 6 fired the first shot at the advancing Custer column. Rowland gave me the names of these guards, but I did not put them down.[18]

Rowland told me of an outpost of Indians some twenty miles out from the Little Big Horn river, who discovered the approach of Custer.[19]

Rowland further stated [that] the man seen by the Indians among Custer's men, who was dressed in the buckskin suit, had short hair; and as the Indians knew Custer as Long Hair, they did not think the man with the buckskin suit was the General. The fact is that Custer went out from Fort Lincoln on this expedition with his hair cut—another circumstance suggesting that the man in buckskin was in reality Gen. Custer.

---

[16]Cheyenne directional orientations do not confirm with the magnetic compass directions. According to the map herein, which was probably drawn by Willis Rowland, the Cheyenne *north* pertains to the area behind Custer Ridge, where I Company was destroyed. This location would be identified on the compass as north/northeast, but is more commonly spoken of by whites as an east location.

[17]The question of drunkenness among the troops was initially raised by two Cheyennes, Two Moons and Wooden Leg, whose statements were later discredited through the investigatory efforts of John Stands in Timber and Dr. Thomas B. Marquis. The latter, who gave this matter his special attention, concluded that whiskey did not influence the conduct of Custer's soldiers that day, and that this whole matter had too thin a foundation to give serious consideration. Yet, this accusation should not be discounted altogether because Lakotas interviewed by Walter Campbell, and the Red Feather interview hereafter, confirm Two Moon's statement.

[18]The two Cheyennes referred to may have been Bobtail Horse, a member of the Elk Scrapers Society, and Roan Bear, a Kit Fox warrior.

[19]According to the Minneconjou, White Bull, Custer's troops were discovered as early as June 22 while leaving the Yellowstone. In addition, the Lakota, Owns Bobtail Horse, and two companions saw Custer's force near the vacated Sundance camp on the Rosebud on June 24. Outriders of a small band of Little Wolf's Cheyennes also saw Custer's soldiers on the Rosebud, and followed them from the present town of Busby to the Little Bighorn. And lastly, the village was warned in advance about the coming of soldiers by a Cheyenne prophet named Old Brave Wolf.

The Red Feather Interview

Editorial note: The Red Feather interview is contained in a feature article printed in the *Daily* (Sioux Falls) *Argus Leader*, issue of July 20, 1925, of which a clipping is in the author's collection.

Red Feather was born about 1855 and was the son of Old Red Feather of Big Road's Oglala band of Bad Faces. Red Feather, also known as Emil Red Feather, was a brother-in-law of the Oglala leader Crazy Horse. The interview which follows was conducted by Cora Babbitt Johnson, a feature writer for the *Argus Leader*. At the time of the interview, Red Feather was convalescing from a leg amputation performed at the Hot Springs Hospital in South Dakota. The translation was rendered by Stanley Red Feather, an educated full blood who was Emil's son. For another interview with Red Feather, see his account in Hardorff, *Lakota Recollections*, pp. 80–88. The text which follows has been divided into paragraphs.

Hot Springs, South Dakota
[July, 1925]

I am an Oglala Sioux and at the time of the fight I was 21 years old. Crazy Horse was the leader of the Oglalas; my sister was his wife.[1] There were a good many thousand Indians who were all together near the Yellowstone river. Usually we scattered at that time of the year, but we had heard the white men were coming to fight us and we all stayed together.

We were camping in the bed of a creek, beyond the river. I don't know how many there were in all, but in the band I belonged to there were about a thousand young men and a good many old ones; I don't know how many.[2]

We did not know the soldiers were so near, and the morning they attacked us I was asleep in my tent. The sun was quite high, but I was sleepy and I came near sleeping too long to get into the fight.[3]

One of our men who had been watching outside the camp rode in with a bunch of horses he had rounded up, and rode from tent to tent, telling us that the soldiers were coming. When I heard him I didn't believe him and I didn't get up for a while; when I did, the soldiers were almost upon us.

They didn't have any chance; they were just a little band and we were thousands. We have always thought Custer was either crazy or drunk to attack us without knowing more about our camp. But maybe he wanted to be made a higher officer and he would take a big chance. He would have been brave to fight the way he did if we had attacked him, but I don't know what to call it the way they attacked us.

It was about 10 o'clock when they charged into our camp, but soon everyone was killed.

I saw one soldier escape on a sorrel horse. I saw him again a

---

[1]The name of Red Feather's sister was Black Shawl who married Crazy Horse in 1870.

[2]This total is too high. According to the Oglala, Red Hawk, the Oglala camp at the Little Bighorn contained 350 warriors. A census of Crazy Horse's band at the surrender in May of 1877 seems to support this lower total. The count reported a total of 145 lodges, with a population of 217 men, 212 women, 186 boys, and 184 girls.

[3]Red Feather stayed up late to attend the social dances held on the evening of June 24. These events offered young men the opportunity to socialize with the girls.

long way off and I saw a puff of smoke near him, but I don't know what became of him. Some Cheyenne Indians chased his horse, but their horses were almost worn out, but they got his horse. They never found him, alive or dead.[4]

On a hill, quite a way off, there were seven or eight men in a bunch, and southeast of the main fight there were some men fighting behind wagons.[5] Some Indians came and fought with them; I think they killed them all. But there were a few others who got away.

On a ridge of hills there were some men fighting hand to hand with Indians. Maybe one of them was General Custer. But we never knew for sure which one he was. I have seen pictures which show him with long hair, but I know he did not have long hair, for if he had he would have been scalped.

We didn't find anyone who looked as Custer had been described, except that there was one man with a buckskin uniform, and other who had yellow stripes on his uniform and ornaments on his shoulders and a buckskin jacket.[6] We thought one of them might have been Custer.

Each soldier carried a knapsack.[7] On one side of each knapsack was found a piece of bacon and crackers. On the other side there were oats and a canteen. The canteens were nearly empty; some of them were entirely empty. I didn't know then what whiskey smelled like, but now I think the strange smell that came from the canteens was whiskey. There was only —— [illegible][8] killed in my band.

---

[4]Red Feather stated in an earlier account that this soldier shot himself and fell from his horse, and that this horse was captured by a Hunkpapa.

[5]This statement has reference to the fight on Reno Hill where soldiers fought from behind a barricade of cracker boxes, which the Indians referred to as wagon boxes.

[6]A total of six officers could fit this description: Yates, Keogh, Calhoun, Porter, Smith, and Cooke, who all wore buckskin jackets and blue trousers with yellow stripes.

[7]Red Feather probably means saddlebags.

[8]Unfortunately, the number is missing because of a tear in the clipping. However, other Lakota sources place the Oglala dead count at five, namely Bad Light Hair, Many Lice, White Eagle, Young Skunk, and Black White Man who died later from his wounds.

The Old Bull Statement

Editorial note: The Old Bull statement is housed in the Walter Stanley Campbell Collection, Box 105, Notebook 11, pp. 13–14, Western History Collections, University of Oklahoma. It is reproduced hereafter with their permission.

Born of Hunkpapa-Yanktonai parents, Old Bull was a member of the Fox Warrior Society, and was said to have been an aide-de-camp to Chief Sitting Bull. After the surrender of the Sioux, Old Bull enlisted with the Standing Rock Agency Police, but resigned for philosophical differences with the Indian Agent just prior to the killing of Sitting Bull. Listed on the Agency rolls as Moses Old Bull, he was gifted with an excellent, retentive memory and became known as a living repository of Hunkpapa tribal history. This interview, which is part of a much larger narrative, was obtained by Walter Campbell during his sweeping field research in North Dakota, Montana, and Canada, in 1928.

[Fort Yates, North Dakota]
[Spring, 1928]

Reno Fight. I was there. Sioux tribe got many guns [from

Custer's battlefield], and surround wagons[1] and fire at them from every side.

[A] fellow [named] Dog's Back was yelling, "Be careful— it is a long way from here but their bullets are coming fierce." As he finishes, [he] gets shot in [the] head and [was] killed.[2] [This took place] in [the] middle [of the] day, day after Custer [was] killed [and] five miles from where Custer [was] killed, southeast [of Custer] and ¼ mile [from] Greasy Grass—Greasy Grass runs north and south [here, and] this [happened] on east side. Breech Cloth was killed there [also].[3]

[In the] middle of the day [on June 26], [during] north side shooting, Sitting Bull says, "Leave 'em go now so some can go home and spread the news. I just saw some more soldiers coming."[4] [The] fight started early in the day, but Old Bull didn't arrive till midday, about closing time.

[Soldiers] on ridge dug [a] trench on side of north hill. Wagons [had been] placed in straight line. Dead horses used as fort in shape of corral.

Soldiers made mistake [by] attacking Hunkpapas first.

---

[1]This is another reference to the barricade of cracker boxes, which looked like wagon beds.

[2]*Sunka Cancohan* 'Dog's Backbone' was a Minneconjou Lakota who was killed by a gunshot to the forehead on June 26.

[3]Breech Cloth was a young Lakota who was shot east of Reno Hill while charging in front of the soldiers near dusk on June 25.

[4]This was the Montana column which went into bivouac near the present site of Crow Agency on June 26.

The Flying Hawk Narrative

Editorial note: The Flying Hawk narrative is contained in M. I. McCreight, *Firewater and Forked Tongues* (Trail's End Publishing Co.: Pasadena, CA, 1947), pp. 111–15.

Flying Hawk (1852–1931) was the son of the Oglala, Black Fox, and the Hunkpapa, Iron Cedar Woman, a sister of Sitting Bull. Flying Hawk's brother was Kicking Bear who is chiefly remembered for his fanatical leadership during the Ghost Dance troubles of 1890. Flying Hawk married two sisters, named White Day and Goes Out Looking, of which the latter bore him a son known as Felix. Flying Hawk died on Christmas Eve, 1931, allegedly from starvation. For another account by Flying Hawk, see Hardorff, *Lakota Recollections of the Custer Fight*, pp. 49–55. M. I. McCreight was an Easterner who was sympathetic to the plight of the Sioux.

[DuBois, Pennsylvania, 1928]

The Indians were camped along the west side of the Big Horn in a flat valley. We saw a dust but did not know what caused it. Some Indians said it was the soldiers coming. The Chief saw a flag on a pole on the hill.

The soldiers made a long line and fired into our tepees

among our women and children. That was the first we knew of any trouble. The women got their children by the hand and caught up their babies and ran in every direction.

The Indian men got their horses and guns as quick as they could and went after the soldiers. Kicking Bear and Crazy Horse were in the lead.[1] There was the thick timber, and when they [Reno's soldiers] got out of the timber, there was where the first of the fight was.

The dust was thick and we could hardly see. We got right among the soldiers and killed a lot with our bows and arrows and tomahawks. Crazy Horse was ahead of all, and he killed a lot of them with his war club; he pulled them off their horses when they tried to get across the river where the bank was steep. Kicking Bear was right beside him and killed many, too, in the water.

This fight was in the upper part of the valley where most of the Indians were camped. It was some of the Reno soldiers that came after us there. It was in the day just before dinner when the soldiers attacked us. When we went after them they tried to run into the timber and get over the water where they had left their wagons.[2] The bank was about this high (12 feet indicated) and steep, and they got off their horses and tried to climb out of the water on their hands and knees, but we killed nearly all of them when they were running through the woods and in the water. The ones that got across the river and up the hill dug holes and stayed in them.

The soldiers that were on the hill with packhorses began to fire on us. About this time all the Indians had got their horses and guns and bows and arrows and war clubs, and they charged the soldiers in the east and north on top of the

---

[1]Crazy Horse and his followers joined late in the Reno Fight. The delay was caused by Crazy Horse's lengthy incantations to invoke the spirit powers for himself and his pony. According to the Oglalas, these rites had taken so much time that the young men of his band were barely able to restrain their impatience.

[2]Like others, Flying Hawk mistook the barricade of cracker boxes for wagon boxes.

hill. Custer was farther north than these soldiers were then. He was going to attack the lower end of the village. We drove nearly all that got away from us down the hill along the ridge where another lot of soldiers were trying to make a stand.[3]

Crazy Horse and I left the crowd and rode down along the river. We came to a ravine; then we followed up the gulch to a place in the rear of the soldiers that were making the stand on the hill.[4] Crazy Horse gave his horse to me to hold along with my horse. He crawled up the ravine to where he could see the soldiers. He shot them as fast as he could load his gun. They fell off their horses as fast as he could shoot. (Here the Chief swayed rapidly back and forth to show how fast they fell.) When they found they were being killed so fast, the ones that were left broke and ran as fast as their horses could go to some other soldiers that were further along the ridge toward Custer. Here they tried to make another stand and fired some shots, but we rushed them on along the ridge to where Custer was. Then they made another stand (the third) and rallied a few minutes. Then they went on along the ridge and got with Custer's men.

Other Indians came to us after we got most of the men at the ravine. We all kept after them until they got to where Custer was. There was only a few of them left then.

By that time all the Indians in the village had got their horses and guns and watched Custer. When Custer got nearly to the lower end of the camp, he started to go down a gulch, but the Indians were surrounding him, and he tried to fight. They got off their horses and made a stand, but it was no use. Their horses ran down the ravine right into the vil-

---

[3]The text is not clear whether this observation pertains to Reno's retreat from the valley, or whether it is a reference to Weir's retreat from Weir Point.

[4]This may have been Deep Ravine, or Crazy Horse Gully as it is known in Walter Camp's notes. This course would have taken Crazy Horse into Calhoun Coulee behind Calhoun Ridge where the led horses were sheltered.

lage. The squaws caught them as fast as they came. One of them was a sorrel with white stockings. Long time after, some of our relatives told us they had seen Custer on that kind of a horse when he was on the way to the Big Horn.

When we got them surrounded the fight was over in one hour. There was so much dust we could not see much, but the Indians rode around and yelled the war whoop and shot into the soldiers as fast as they could until they were all dead. One soldier was running away to the east, but Crazy Horse saw him and jumped on his pony and went after him. He got him about half a mile from the place where the others were lying dead. The smoke was lifted so we could see a little. We got off our horses and went and took the rings and money and watches from the soldiers. We took some clothes off, too, and all the guns and pistols. We got seven hundred guns and pistols. Then we went back to the women and children and got them together that were not killed or hurt.

It was hard to hear the women singing the death song for the men killed, and for the wailing, because their children were shot while they played in the camp. It was a big fight; the soldiers got just what they deserved this time. No good soldiers would shoot into the Indian's tepee where there were women and children. These soldiers did, and we fought for our women and children. White men would do the same if they were men.

We did not mutilate the bodies, but just took the valuable things we wanted and then left. We got a lot of money, but it was of no use.

We got our things packed up and took care of the wounded the best we could, and left there the next day. We could have killed all the men that got into the holes on the hill, but they were glad to let us alone, and so we let them alone, too. Rain-in-the-Face was with me in the fight. There were twelve hundred of us. Might be no more than one thousand in the fight.[5] Many of our Indians were out on a hunt.

There was more than one Chief in the fight, but Crazy Horse was leader and did most to win the fight, along with Kicking Bear. Sitting Bull was right with us. His part in the fight was all good. My mother and Sitting Bull's wife were sisters; she is still living.

The names of the chiefs in the fights were: Crazy Horse, Sitting Bull, Lame Deer, Spotted Eagle[6] and Two Moon. Two Moon led the Cheyennes. Gall and some other chiefs were there, but the ones I told you were the leaders. The story that white men told about Custer's heart being cut out is not true.

---

[5]According to Custer scholar John S. Gray, the total Indian population of the Little Bighorn village consisted of 1,000 lodges, containing 7,120 persons, including 1,780 males. However, Gray's contemporary, Robert A. Marshall, estimated a ceiling of 795 lodges with a corresponding population of 5,056 persons. These totals differ sharply from the estimate given by the Minneconjou, White Bull, whose interview is published herein.

[6]Spotted Eagle was the prominent leader of a Northern Sans Arc band. He was known among his people as a traditionalist and preferred exile in Canada over reservation life in the U.S. After Spotted Eagle's surrender in 1879, his band settled on the Cheyenne River Agency where he died in 1898.

The Young Eagle Statement

Editorial note: The Young Eagle statement is housed in the Walter Stanley Campbell Collection, Box 105, Notebook 32, pp. 42–44, Western History Collections, University of Oklahoma. It is reproduced hereafter with their permission.

Young Eagle, also known as Callous Leg, was born about 1859. After the surrender of Sitting Bull's band in 1881, Young Eagle enlisted with the Standing Rock Indian Police and was on duty during the arrest and killing of Sitting Bull in 1890. Young Eagle had a son named Edward. This statement was obtained by Walter Campbell on September 2, 1929, when he managed to interview ten elderly Lakota warriors in one day. During that year Campbell conducted research among the Sioux, Cheyennes, and Crows.

[Fort Yates, North Dakota]
[September 2, 1929]

Callous Leg, or, Young Eagle, [is] 70 [years of age] and doesn't show [his] age [and is] all talk! [He was] always with Sitting Bull's band. [He was] 17 [years old] in Custer massacre [and with] Sitting Bull's band.

Sitting Bull [was] not in [the] battle, but [was] on [the]

warpath against [the] Crows in [the] Little Big Horn Mountains—not in Custer massacre. . . .[1] Young Eagle went to Canada with Sitting Bull after [the] Little Bighorn battle, to the foothills of [the] Rockies. Sitting Bull liked and stole horses. [He] had over one hundred, more or less.

Custer [Fight.] Young Eagle assures he is telling the truth. [I] don't think Sitting Bull took part [in fight with Custer], but [the Hunkpapa] outfit did. [I] don't think Sitting Bull took part even with Reno [fight].

Young Eagle fought on [the] side of [Calhoun] hill. Custer's men went behind [the] ridge and Indians got off [their] horses and fought [the soldiers]. Gall, [who was] Young Eagle's half brother, [was the] leader of the fight.

After Custer [went] over [the] ridge, [we] saw one man to every three horses.[2] Indians surrounded whites on horses. Very few Indians had guns; most had arrows and tomahawks. [The] whites [were] good fighters. Young Eagle killed several.

---

[1]Young Eagle is mistaken because Sitting Bull's presence at the battle is clearly established by his relatives and other contemporaries.

[2]Cavalry companies were divided in sets of fours, and when ordered to dismount and fight on foot, the horses of each set were held by one trooper, freeing the other three soldiers for combat activities. Considering the stresses caused by combat noise, it would have been virtually impossible for one man to control four horses by merely holding them by their reins. For that reason, a bridle was supplied with a strap on each side, along with a snap ring, which allowed the holder to link the four horses together.

The Gray Whirlwind Interview

Editorial note: The Gray Whirlwind statement is housed in the Walter Stanley Campbell Collection, Box 105, Notebook 14, pp. 11–15, Western History Collections, University of Oklahoma. It is reproduced hereafter with their permission.

Gray Whirlwind was born about 1840 and was the son of the Yanktonai, Two Bears. This statement was obtained by Walter Campbell on September 2, 1929, when he interviewed ten elderly Lakota warriors in one day.

[Fort Yates, North Dakota]
[September 2, 1929]

[He is] 89 [years old]. Soldiers [were] first [seen] on ridge. We see [the] dust [only]. No soldiers there. Scouts return and say, "Whole American army [is] coming." Sitting Bull says, "I don't want my children to fight until I tell them to. That army may be com[ing] to make peace, or be officials bringing rations to us."[1]

---

[1]Incredible as this statement may sound, other Lakota warriors expressed similar sentiments on this matter. The Minneconjou, Feather Earring, and the Oglala, He Dog, both told Gen. Hugh L. Scott that the Indians could have been led into their agencies without a fight if Custer had called for a council instead of resorting to armed confrontation.

Reno deployed [his] men. Sitting Bull's horse [was] shot in two places, and Sitting Bull said, "Now my best horse is shot; it is like they have shot me; attack them." Rain in the Face leads against Reno.

On [the] n[orth] side [other] soldiers come again (Custer). Sitting Bull said, "These soldiers fought us so those [warriors] may attack them (Custer). One [soldier] on [a] sorrel horse tries to get away and does from the [main] command. As he gets over [a] ridge, two Santee boys chase him and knock him off [his] horse and take [his] horse.

When [the] warriors cross [the] river, they wait up [a] coulee for Sitting Bull to catch up [and] to attack Custer. Gray Whirlwind was there. [Also the] son of Red Staff, Holy Cloud, [and] Iron Bear, [all of the] Yanktonai [tribe]. Yankton and Sitting Bull's outfits [were] all over hunting and thus together. Above three [were] with Gray Whirlwind and saw above.

When Sitting Bull arrived [he did] not [go into battle], but told them to go on and fight. Sitting Bull's horse [was a] sorrel [with a] big tail [and] bald face. Sitting Bull's horse (shot in Reno fight) [was] gray.

[Did] Sitting Bull ride other horses that day?

Don't know. Maybe [a] Crow horse or [a] soldier's horse. Sitting Bull had many himself.

[Did you] see Sitting Bull again that day?

No. We broke camp that evening and different bands [went in] different directions.

What [do you] think of Sitting Bull?

Brave [and] deep thinker.

The White Cow Walking Interview

Editorial note: The White Cow Walking interview is housed in the Walter Stanley Campbell Collection, Box 105, Notebook 32, pp. 56–59, Western History Collections, University of Oklahoma. It is reproduced hereafter with their permission.

White Cow Walking was born about 1849 and was the son of the Oglala chief Horned Horse whose account of the Custer battle is printed herein. The statement which follows was obtained by Walter Camp on September 2, 1929.

[Fort Yates, North Dakota]
[September 2, 1929]

White Cow Walking [is] 80 [years old]. [He was] in Sitting Bull's band all [the] time. All of Sitting Bull's band went to Canada. Part returned and came to Standing Rock. White Cow Walking stayed in Canada. [He] does not know why, but after the Custer massacre Gall came back [to Standing Rock] and Sitting Bull went on. Gall didn't want to fight [any]more.[1]

---

[1]Due to their impoverished living conditions in Canada, Gall's Hunkpapa band of 300 people surrendered to Major Hugo Ilges at Camp Poplar, Wyoming Territory, on January 2, 1881. Sitting Bull and 188 of his followers crossed the border six months later and surrendered to Major David S. Brotherton at Fort Bufort, Dakota Territory, on July 19, 1881.

Sitting Bull took part in [the] fight with Custer and Reno. Some [Indians had] arrows and tomahawks, [and] some [had] guns. [He] doesn't know what Sitting Bull had. A coup counted as [a] mixup [occurred].

When Custer appeared, [there was a] call for Indians to wait. Soldiers shot first. Sitting Bull and some women fought Reno [and] then Custer. It was foretold [about the battle], but [it was] not known whether Sitting Bull's [vision was correct] or not. [We were] not prepared or camped to fight. . . .

[White Cow Walking] took part in [the] Little Big Horn [fight] and [the] Bear Coat [fight],[2] but [he was] young [then]. [He] doubts Sitting Bull's presence [at the fighting]. [He] was told [that] Sitting Bull [was] in [the] sun dance at age of 50. [He] doubts [the] part Sitting Bull took [in it]; but all [men] at age 40 to 50 who took [part in the] sun dance in Montana pierced [themselves].

White Cow Walking took part [in the Custer Fight] and

---

[2]Bear Coat was the Indian name for Gen. Nelson A. Miles. The Bear Coat Fight took place in January 1877. The *Record of Engagements with Hostile Indians* discloses that: "on the 29th of December [of 1876] Colonel Miles, with Companies A, C, D, E, and K, Fifth Infantry, and Companies E and F, Twenty-Second Infantry, numbering 436 officers and men, with two pieces of artillery, moved out against the Sioux and Cheyennes under Crazy Horse, whose camp had been reported south of the Yellowstone, in the valley of Tongue River. As the column moved up the Tongue the Indians abandoned their winter camps, consisting of about 600 lodges, and the column had two sharp skirmishes on the 1st and 3d of January [1877], driving the Indians up the valley of Tongue River, until the night of the 7th, when the advance captured a young warrior and seven Cheyenne women and children, who proved to be relatives of one of the headmen of the tribe. A determined attempt was made by the Indians to rescue the prisoners, and preparations were made for a severe fight to be expected the next day. On the morning of January 8, about 600 warriors appeared in front of the troops and an engagement followed, lasting about five hours. The fight took place in a canyon, the Indians occupying a spur of the Wolf Mountain range, from which they were driven by repeated charges. The ground was covered with ice and snow to a depth of from one to three feet, and the latter portion of the engagement was fought in a blinding snowstorm, the troops stumbling and falling in scaling the ice and snow covered cliffs from which the Indians were driven, with serious loss in killed and wounded, through the Wolf Mountains and in the direction of the Big Horn range." The Indians' loss amounted to one Cheyenne and two Lakotas. The names of the captured Cheyennes referred to were Big Horse, Sweet Woman, Roman Nose Woman (Wooden Leg's sister), Twin Woman (Lame White Man's widow), and the wife of Little Chief, along with three children.

will tell [about] Custer's massacre [in which he] counted coup. [His] brother [was] scalped and killed by Reno [soldiers].[3]

[He did] not [fight] beside Sitting Bull, but [he] thinks Sitting Bull counted coup [just] as all [other] warriors.

White Cow Walking was [an] Oglala under Red Cloud [and] in [the] Little Big Horn battle [fought] with Sitting Bull. Red Cloud [was] not in Little Big Horn [fight]. White Cow Walking [was] away from council of Sitting Bull's peace.

[When] Custer soldiers first appeared Gall told Indians to wait [with the attack] to protect [the] women and children; then [the] soldiers fired into them, and they killed [the] soldiers all along [Calhoun] ridge. . . .

Did [you] expect Custer?

Didn't know for sure, but [we] thought Custer [was] stationed there.

White Cow Walking [was] in Custer fight and came back, and [then] heard of soldiers (Reno) [on hill to the] south and went that way. [He] brought able-bodied horses. Lots of Indians [had been] killed. [He] had bow and arrows [and was] on horseback. [He had] shot and killed Crow Flies High, [a] soldier scout.[4]

Many [captured] guns [were] loaded and [had] not [been] shot. [There was] too much confusion to say [the] number of whites killed by clubs. [They had] camped one day before Custer came. [He] heard of [the] sun dance [on the Rosebud], but [did] not attend. [He] heard of Sitting Bull speeches and forecasting, but [he was] with Oglalas.

---

[3]The name of this brother was White Eagle, the only Oglala killed during the Reno Fight. He was slain on the west slope of Reno Hill during the pursuit of the retreating troopers and was scalped by Pvt. John W. Wallace of G Company. White Eagle's body was recovered after dark by White Cow Walking.

[4]The soldier scout Crow Flies High was probably the Lakota name for one of the three Ree Indian Scouts killed with Reno: either Sgt. Bobtail Bull, Bloody Knife, or Little Soldier (aka Little Brave, Stub, and Bear's Trail). It is possible that the name might have referred to Michel Bouyer, or Isaiah Dorman. However, Bouyer was already known by the Lakota name of *Kapi* 'Hammering Out' (as in the pounding iron by a blacksmith), while Dorman was known as *Azi* 'Teats' for his conspicuous dark-brown nipples.

The One Bull Interview

Editorial note: The One Bull Interview is housed in the Walter Stanley Campbell Collection, Box 105, Notebook 19, pp. 37–47, Western History Collections, University of Oklahoma. It is reproduced hereafter with their permission.

Tatanka winjila 'One Bull,' or 'Lone Bull,' better known to the whites as Henry Oscar One Bull (1853–1947), was the son of the Minneconjou band chief Makes Room and Pretty Feather Woman, a sister of the Hunkpapa chief Sitting Bull. At age four One Bull was adopted by Sitting Bull and eventually became a member of his bodyguard. He was a member of the Fox Warrior Society, and after the surrender of Sitting Bull's band in 1881, he enlisted with the Standing Rock Indian Police and served until 1890. One Bull was married to the Hunkpapa woman Red Whirlwind and lies buried next to her in the mission cemetery on Little Oak Creek, near Little Eagle, South Dakota. One Bull was a full brother of White Bull whose interview is printed herein. The interview which follows was conducted by Walter S. Campbell during his second visit with One Bull's family in 1929.

[Grand River, near Little Eagle, South Dakota]
[September 3, 1929]

1. Horseman from south reports soldiers coming
2. Deeds, brother of Hona[1]
3. Indians could see dust
4. Soldiers
5. Second line skirmished on horseback

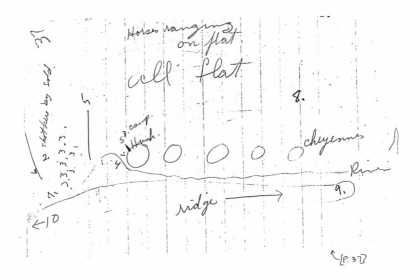

One Bull and Gray Eagle[2] had been [out] to get [grazing] horses. When [they came] back to Sitting Bull's tent, [someone] tells [that a] boy [was] killed, and [then] soldiers arrive

---

[1]Deeds was a Hunkpapa boy who was killed shortly before the commencement of the valley fight. He was a brother of *Hona* 'Little Voice,' whose statement is published hereafter.

[2]Born about 1851, Gray Eagle, aka Gabriel Gray Eagle, was the son of Old Gray Eagle and Shell Woman, both Hunkpapas. Gray Eagle's sisters were Seen By Her Nation and Four Robes Woman who married Sitting Bull in 1869. After the surrender of the Hunkpapas in 1881, Gray Eagle enlisted as a U.S. Indian Scout and was present during the killing of Sitting Bull in 1890. Gray Eagle was later appointed Judge of the Court of Indian Offenses at Standing Rock and served honorably for many years.

[and] start shooting. Women and children ran north to other camps.

When shooting starts, One Bull gives his gun to Sitting Bull, and takes his bow and arrows and pogamoggan [war club] and Sitting Bull's shield. Indians had to stay low— [they were] not on ridge.

Soldiers leave horses at "4" on flat in bend of river. Indians [congregate] along creek. One Bull tells [them], "[We] need all take a —— [missing word]."

One Bull starts south after [the] soldiers. When in view [of them he] says, "Have mercy on me God [*Wakan Tanka*], that [I may] have no sin." One Bull is followed by White Bull, brother [of] Crow King, [and] Black Moon [and] Swift Bear, [the latter also a] brother [of] Crow King.[3] Both flanks [of soldiers' skirmish line] retreat, [but] middle [of line] stands, [and] they retreat last.

Good Bear Boy [is] shot and wounded and falls on bank. Soldiers [turn] back and Indians go around bend in river. One Bull goes back for Good Bear Boy who was shot in [the] leg and helps him [mount] on [One Bull's] horse. One Bull then leads [the] horse back to camp, going backwards to hide himself [behind the horse].[4]

Then soldiers [mount] on horses and line up [at] "5". One Bull [is] on [retreat] behind wounded man and goes south-west. When [the] horse turned around for One Bull to get on, horse [gets] shot in hip. Then fight at "5" [takes place]. When White Bull arrives [at a place of safety he] pulls [the] wounded man off [his horse and leaves him] for others to get as his horse limps.

----

[3]White Bull, Swift Bear, and Black Moon, all Hunkpapas, were killed during Reno's valley fight.

[4]Good Bear Boy was a young Hunkpapa who sustained a gunshot to his left leg, which broke the bone. He was rescued by One Bull who tied a rawhide rope around the wounded boy's chest and dragged him out of the immediate line of firing. Good Bear Boy recovered from his injury and died a natural death at Standing Rock Agency many years later.

From Sitting Bull's camp to "6" where soldiers recrossed [is] five miles, or maybe less. Few soldiers got to river. One Bull kills two in [the] river and one across [the] river. Then Sitting Bull arrives on east side and tells One Bull to quit. Sitting Bull says [that] One Bull [was] well spent, seeing [the] blood [on his chest]. Then One Bull tells [him that it was the] wounded man's blood.

Only four soldiers [are] alive across [the] river at "7", and One Bull and another [warrior] start after [them], but [then] Sitting Bull says not [to follow them, but to] let them go back to tell [the story]. But One Bull and the other [warrior] follow the four [soldiers] up [the] bluff [and onto the] ridge [and when] on top [they] see pack mules south of [the] mouth of creek [that runs] from [the] east.

Then [the] Indians gather [at] north end [of the] camp after [Reno's] fight [is] over. When at [the] north end, [they] see another troop coming down the ridge—[going] north. One Bull starts to go [towards them], but Sitting Bull says [there are] enough [Indians] there now—no need to go.

Sitting Bull [then went] from Reno's field to west [side] of Cheyenne [village], looking north, on flat west of camp, at "8". No one [of Sitting Bull's party] climbed [the] hill[;] ([stayed on] river bench). Sitting Bull [was] about two miles from [the] fighting [with Custer] at [that] time. Many [people were] at "8" near Sitting Bull and [were] not in [the] fight. Fight on [Custer] hill [at] "9" [lasted] *about one hour* [italics in original]. Sitting Bull and One Bull gathered with rest at north end of camp. [They] didn't go over to [see the] dead.

[Did] whites at "10" on [Reno] hill stay several days? [They] leave [the] second night.

[Did the Indians] try to get mules? Yes. One Bull [was] not there. Sitting Bull met others returning with pack mules about east [of] "5".

First day after fight [they] stayed as [they] heard other soldiers were coming and [they] got [the] above mules.[5] [They]
moved camp near "5" when [they] heard [that] soldiers were
coming.

[Did] Sitting Bull ask them not to kill men on [Reno] hill?
Yes, [but] while [Sitting Bull was] telling [this], one Indian
[was] shot in [the] head, a Minneconjou. [His name was]
'Sunka cancohan nata ataya opi.'[6] His son's name [is] King
Man [who lives] at Cheyenne Agency. After [this death] Sit-
ting Bull tells One Bull not to go east from "8" to fight.

[Sitting Bull] had [a] dream over [the] fight [while] in
sundance on Rosebud and told them they would kill soldiers,
but [he warned], "Do not touch their bodies [and] don't take
the spoils." Announcer Black Moon[7] announced [this] for
him. After [the] battle [there was] much am[munition] left,
but Sitting Bull nor his band would not touch [the] spoils.

---

[5]This statement is corroborated by the Cheyenne, Wooden Leg. The mule train
was commanded by Lt. Edward G. Mathey and consisted of 174 pack mules, including
thirteen which carried the reserve ammunition of the regiment. Soon after the pack
train's arrival on Reno Hill, some of these mules started to stray from the packers,
including several ammo mules. The subsequent antics of one of these ammo mules,
named Old Barnum, earned Mathey a severe tongue lashing from Capt. Benteen,
while Sgt. Richard P. Hanley, who caught Old Barnum just in time, was awarded a
Medal of Honor. Unfortunately, Pvt. John B. McGuire, who assisted Hanley, failed
to receive any recognition at all. In addition to Old Barnum, it appears that a second
ammo mule strayed from Reno Hill. This mule apparently wandered to the river
where the Indians captured him and relieved him of his valuable burden.

[6]This is another reference to Spinal Bone of a Dog, or Dog's Backbone, who was
killed on the north side of Reno Hill on June 26.

[7]This was the Hunkpapa, Old Black Moon, who was an uncle of Sitting Bull. Old
Black Moon's son, Young Black Moon, was the head soldier of the Hunkpapa camp
police and was killed during the opening phase of the valley fight.

The Turning Hawk Interview

Editorial note: The Turning Hawk interview is housed in the Walter Stanley Campbell Collection, Box 105, Notebook 38, pp. 13–21, Western History Collections, University of Oklahoma. It is reproduced hereafter with their permission.

Turning Hawk, or Circling Hawk, was a renowned Hunkpapa who had a reputation for prowess and was held in considerable esteem among his fellow tribesmen. Turning Hawk's name is mentioned as early as 1868 when he was identified as the Pipe Bearer (leader) of a war party, among whom was Sitting Bull himself. Turning Hawk was a member of the respected Silent Eaters Society. The interview which follows was conducted by Walter Campbell during his field research in the Dakotas, Montana, and Canada, in 1930.

[Fort Yates, North Dakota]
[June 1930]

Turning Hawk [came] from north and [at] "4" got along [the] river.[1] Turning Hawk [was almost] killed [at] "5" in

---

[1]The numbers in the text have reference to a map which, unfortunately, is missing from the interview pages. However, the reader is referred to the One Bull map in the preceding interview because the orientation numbers mentioned on that map correspond well with the orientation numbers in the Turning Hawk text.

Custer massacre, but came alive again. Three [of us] went after Custer [Reno's] horses and two [were] killed, but [the] bullets flying around [at] "5" did not hit Turning Hawk.

[There were] three companies. Turning Hawk [was] in party behind army [Reno?]. Turning Hawk killed two Indian scouts [at] "6"—one Sioux and one Crow.[2]

[At] "7" Cheyennes ran Reno from water. Reno tried to cross [the] stream. Turning Hawk [was] not with Sitting Bull. [At] "6" [were enemy scouts] who were trying to run off horses.[3] When so many [soldiers were] killed, Reno tried to get away, but [at] "7" several soldiers dropped in [the] river.

Turning Hawk had lots of bullets, and was in [a] Canadian fight one time with Sitting Bull.

Turning Hawk shot a cavalryman, and [the] horse fell on [the] cavalryman, and Turning Hawk thought the cavalryman [was] dead. Turning Hawk rushed into [the] middle of the battle [with two others to coup the soldier], and [these] two [others were] shot down.

Sitting Bull [was] not in [battle at] "9", but [was] with [others who confronted] Custer [Reno?]. Arapahoes and Cheyennes at "7", and Turning Hawk [was] there. Sitting Bull just [got] back from Crow Reservation when Custer massacre [took place].

Turning Hawk said [he almost] died as four [Indians] rushed into battle and three [were] killed.[4] Turning Hawk

---

[2]No Crow Scouts were killed in the valley fight. However, White Swan was severely wounded on the east bank of the river and was found lying on his back when rescued by the other scouts. It is possible that White Swan was shot by Turning Hawk who may have assumed that he had killed the Crow. The slain Sioux scout may have been Bloody Knife who was born from a mixed marriage between a Hunkpapa man and a Ree woman.

[3]On the east side of the river near present Garry Owen, six Ree scouts captured a small herd of twenty-seven ponies and two mules which they drove up the bluffs near Reno Hill. They were hotly pursued by angry Sioux who eventually were able to recover the stolen stock.

[4]This may be a reference to the deaths of White Bull, Swift Bear, and Black Moon. These men were the first to charge Reno's skirmish line along with One Bull, who was the only survivor.

ran into [a] soldier in [the] center of battle and [was] knocked off [his] horse which was taken by Crows.[5] [An enemy] Indian [at] "10" then shot at Turning Hawk. Smoke and dust [were] terrible when [at] "10". Turning Hawk threw himself down. [This] man shot [again] at Turning Hawk, and Turning Hawk hit him in [the] hip and breast, killing him. [This enemy scout] happened to be a Sioux named Brush and [he was a] chief.[6] Then [there was] room for Turning Hawk to run out [of the battle].

Lots of soldiers [were] drunk [at] "11" and shot each other. Some smelt [of liquor] after [their] deaths.[7]

Turning Hawk got [another] horse and returned to [the] fight, [but by then] only [a] few [soldiers were] left. Turning Hawk [was] now with Bad Bear and Little Buffalo. One soldier grabbed Little Buffalo [at] "12", [but] Little Buffalo took [his] bridle and struck [the] soldier and took [his] horse.

---

[5]The Ree Young Hawk later recalled that one Lakota charged the soldiers very closely and was shot about sixteen feet from the skirmish line. This Lakota rode a sorrel pony with a bold face and had his tail knotted with scarlet cloth. When this Lakota fell, his horse kept coming toward the soldiers and was captured by Young Hawk.

[6]The Sioux scout named Brush is not listed on Varnum's muster roll. Among Custer's auxiliary force of Indian Scouts were four Sioux. Two of these were Blackfeet Lakotas, who were brothers, whose names were *Watoksu Mahpiya* 'Ring Cloud,' and *Mato Kinapa* 'Appearing Bear.' The other two scouts were Hunkpapa Lakotas, named *Mahpiya Ska* 'White Cloud,' and *Tatanka Iyapaya* 'Catches Buffalo.' None of these men were killed, or even wounded.

The possibility exists that the victim identified by Turning Hawk as Sioux may have been a member of the Ree tribe. Intertribal marriages between Sioux and Rees were not uncommon, and it is possible, therefore, that, in addition to Bloody Knife, one of the other Ree casualties may also have been of mixed blood. This victim may have been identified by one tribe as Sioux, and by the other as Ree, as was the case with Bloody Knife.

I suspect that the Sioux named Brush was known among the Rees as Bobtail Bull. Charging Hawk said that this man was a chief. Bobtail Bull was the head soldier of the Grass Dance Society and the leader of a Ree band, and his tribal standing was high enough to earn him the enlisted rank of sergeant. Could Bobtail Bull have been of Sioux/Ree parentage? Perhaps the answer lies in his ambiguous statement given at the time of his enlistment, when Bobtail Bull said that "he was not a man to change tribes all the time, that he was always an Arickara and respected their chiefs and had served under them gladly."

[7]The numbers "11" and "12" pertain to locations on Custer's battlefield and are absent from One Bull's map, which covers the Reno Fight only.

At Custer's last stand [at] "12", Little Buffalo got Custer's horse, a dark sorrel. Custer had short hair and [we] couldn't recognize him. After [the] battle [we] heard Custer had [a] sorrel horse and thought it [was the horse captured at] "12". Lots of Indians knew this sorrel to be Custer's. All soldiers had blue shirts.

When all [soldiers had been] killed, [there were] five men with Sitting Bull, and all brought [back captured] horses. One [of these was] Old Bull, [and the] second one [was] Gray Eagle [who] started and returned, [but the names of the] third, fourth, and fifth [men were not remembered by Turning Hawk].

Sitting Bull ordered [the Indians] to stop besieging [Reno Hill] and said, "Let them live—they are trying to live. They came against us and we have killed a few." (Reno end [of fight.])

Knife King was Sitting Bull's crier at that time. [At] "13" Knife King was announcing [something] when [a] soldier in [a] ditch raised [up] and shot Knife King in [the] body; but Knife King lived. [This happened at] "13" after Reno was driven back [to the timber].[8]

Sitting Bull ordered not to mutilate Custer, and Sitting Bull looked at [the] dead to find him. Then [he] went to next fight at [the] other end. Custer's packhorses and pack mules (wagon train) which followed was attacked [the] next day.

After [the] battle Turning Hawk was [enlisted as a] government scout.

---

[8]Knife King was an elderly Hunkpapa who was the Camp Crier of Sitting Bull's band. He was shot in front of Reno's skirmish line by a soldier lying behind the wooded bank. The bullet traversed Knife Chief's body, breaking both of his arms and wounding him so severely that he remained lying on the battlefield until it was safe to remove him by pony travois.

The White Hair on Face Statement

Editorial note: The White Hair on Face interview is housed in the Walter Stanley Campbell Collection, Box 105, Notebook 41, pp. 48–51, Western History Collections, University of Oklahoma, and it is reproduced hereafter with their permission.

This statement was obtained by Walter Campbell during his field research in the Dakotas, Montana, and Canada, during the summer of 1930. A subject search failed to locate any data on this Hunkpapa eyewitness.

[Fort Yates, North Dakota]
[June 1930]

Charging Thunder's band [was] called Meat Necklace [Band]. White Hair on Face went to Canada with Charging Thunder, and came back from Canada on boat with Sitting Bull.[1]

[They] came to America with Sitting Bull, and after [hav-

---

[1] This was the steamer *General Sherman* which was boarded by Sitting Bull at Ft. Buford on July 29, 1881, to be transported to Ft. Randall as a prisoner of war. Sitting Bull was released on May 10, 1883, when he was allowed to return to his agency at Standing Rock.

ing been] fired upon and split [they] went back to Canada with Sitting Bull.[2] About 25 lodges [remained] with Sitting Bull [the] last time [they went] to Canada.[3]

Charging Thunder's band was in Little Big Horn [Fight]. Crow [enemy scouts] circled and scared the horses and White Hair on Face.

Sitting Bull told them not to take things belonging to whites, and he [White Hair on Face] fought on foot. [He was] 20 years old. He guarded women and children with [bow and] arrows. He had to leave to get [a] horse as Crows had worked [ahead] and [had] killed [the] guards of [the] horses and got latter and some ammunition in saddlebags.

One Bull [was] with White Hair on Face on horseback. Sitting Bull [was] there also with [them] due to [all the] excitement. Sitting Bull was *in front* [italics in original] of [the] warriors and White Hair [was initially] on foot behind. [There was] no time to listen for Sitting Bull to speak. Gall [was] there on horseback. *Every one* [was] *talking* [italics in original] and [we] could understand no one.

White Hair on Face at front and met [his] mother-in-law, dragging a little girl and [holding] another. He gave them [his] horse—[the] woman [mounted] in [the] middle, the little girl in back and [the] large girl in front. [He] then told them to [go to the] rest of [the] women and [to] hurry.

---

[2]Near the end of 1876, Sitting Bull's band had several skirmishes with troops of the Fifth Infantry. On October 21, 1876, Gen. Nelson A. Miles attacked the Hunkpapas on Cedar Creek, Montana, and drove them in confusion to the south side of the Yellowstone, causing the surrender of some 400 lodges on October 27. On December 7, Lt. F. D. Baldwin engaged Sitting Bull's warriors near the Missouri, striking them again on December 18 when the entire village of 122 lodges was captured, although Sitting Bull's band managed to escape. It has generally been assumed that the Sioux did not cross into Canada until May of 1877. However, White Hair's statement suggests that the Hunkpapas had entered Canada before the skirmishes with the Fifth Infantry took place. His statement receives corroboration from a military report filed by the Seventh Cavalry. This report discloses that troops had made an attempt to surprise a band of Sioux camped near Wolf Point, Montana, but found that the Indians had fled across the Canadian border, some sixty miles away.

[3]Sitting Bull's camp of twenty-five lodges contained 45 men, 67 women, and 73 children, for a total of 185 people who eventually surrendered on July 19, 1881.

The White Bull Interview

Editorial note: The White Bull interview is housed in the Walter Stanley Campbell Collection, Box 105, Notebook 24, pp. 48–90, Western History Collection, University of Oklahoma. It is reproduced hereafter with their permission.

White Bull (1850–1947) was the son of the Minneconjou band chief Makes Room and Pretty Feather Woman, a sister of Sitting Bull. Known among the Lakotas as *Pte San Hunka* 'Lazy White Buffalo,' he is better known to the whites as Joseph White Bull whose warrior life was immortalized by Stanley Vestal (Walter S. Campbell) in *Warpath, the True Story of the Fighting Sioux, Told in a Biography of Chief White Bull* (Boston, 1934). After his surrender at Fort Bennet in 1876, White Bull enlisted with the Cheyenne River Indian Police and served a total of twelve years. He also served as judge on the Cheyenne River Court of Indian Offenses, serving a term of four years. However, the crowning point of his public career came in 1881 when he was elected to the office of Scalp Shirt Wearer to become one of the six civil chiefs who govern the Minneconjou tribe. Perhaps his greatest personal achievement was reached when he learned to write in the Lakota language. White Bull was a brother of One Bull whose interview is printed herein. The interview which follows was conducted by Walter S. Campbell on Cherry Creek, South Dakota, in 1932. I have corrected grammatical errors, changed abbreviations, and added punctuation. For another interview with White Bull, see Hardorff, *Lakota Recollections of the Custer Fight,* pp. 107–26.

[Cheyenne River Reservation, South Dakota] [June 1932]

11TH FIGHT: CUSTER

White Bull [was] with Sans Arc [tribe] instead of Sitting Bull, in own tent with wife[1] and two children; [there] may have been other Hunkpapas [in Sans Arc circle].

Camps there: Cheyennes, Oglalas, Minneconjous, Sans Arc, Hunkpapa, [a] few Blackfeet (in Sitting Bull's band), Two Kettles, [and a] few Brules.

In S. B. lodge just his own family: both wives,[2] two step-sons, [one] a deaf and dumb [named] Blue Mountain[3] and [the other named] Little Soldier,[4] two girls,[5] Sitting Bull [himself], [and] Gray Eagle. Twins,[6] newly born (week old), also in Sitting Bull's tent. Eight [ten] in Sitting Bull's camp.

---

[1]The name of this wife was Holy Lodge, a Sans Arc woman, who was married to White Bull from 1871 until her death in 1894, the union resulting in the birth of two sons. White Bull's lodge consisted of four people: himself, Holy Lodge, their infant son, and a son from a previous marriage with the Sans Arc, Rattle Track Woman. White Bull's matrimonial history included fifteen wives, while four times he tried to have two wives at the same time.

[2]The younger wife, born 1842, was known as *Tashina Topa Win* 'Four Blankets Woman,' and the older one was named *Oyate Wanyankapi Win* 'Seen by Her Nation.' They were the daughters of Old Gray Eagle and Shell Woman, Hunkpapas.

[3]Blue Mountain was the son of Seen by Her Nation from a former marriage, and he was therefore a stepson of Sitting Bull.

[4]Born about 1862, Little Soldier was the son of Four Blanket Woman from a former marriage with the Yanktonai, Tall Soldier. Little Soldier was thus a stepson of Sitting Bull.

[5]The names of these two girls were Standing Holy (1875–1926), daughter of Seen by Her Nation and Sitting Bull, and Many Horses, Sitting Bull's daughter from a prior marriage.

[6]Four Blanket Woman and Seen by Her Nation both had a pair of twins born from their marriage with Sitting Bull. According to Standing Holy, none of these infants reached maturity and all had died by the time Sitting Bull was killed in 1890.

One Bull [was] married at [that] time and camped near Sitting Bull.[7]

[We] had been there two days before [Custer] fight and came from Rosebud and fought there June 17. Five days later move [and] camp on Little Big Horn . . . when Custer came June 25. [We] did not move to fight but to find buffalo and did not find them on Little Big Horn creek. Hunt on Little Big Horn, [and] then go to Rosebud [and] have Sun Dance and fight (Gen. Crook); then go back to Little Big Horn to hunt and don't find them and [later] go to Powder River. [We] did expect soldiers from Three Stars to follow [us], and Indians had scouts behind [to watch them].

What [did you] do two days before . . . [June 25]?

Trying to rest up from last fight, bury [the] dead and tend [to] wounded.

Chiefs in Hunkpapa camp: Four Horns,[8] Black Moon,[9] Long Horn, No Neck, and Red Horn.[10] Each band camps together in circle of Hunkpapas: 1) Two Kettles, 2) Blackfeet, 3) Sitting Bull, 4) Wacandi, 5) Icis, 6) ——— [blank].[11]

Three hundred lodges in Hunkpapa circle that day. Other circles bigger: Oglalas, Cheyennes, Sans Arc, [and] Minneconjous [had each] 400 to 500 lodges, [and] Hunkpapas

---

[7]One Bull, White Bull's brother, was married to the Hunkpapa, Red Whirlwind Woman.

[8]Four Horns aka Moccasin Top (1800–1887) was the older brother of Jumping Bull, who was Sitting Bull's father. He sustained a gunshot wound during the Killdeer Mountain Fight in 1864 and carried the bullet in his body, which was thought to have been the cause of his death.

[9]Black Moon was an uncle of Sitting Bull and acted as his Camp Crier on special occasions. It was said that he was a loquacious man who was fond of joking. He died at Standing Rock Agency in 1888.

[10]This man was said to have instituted the *Ska Yuha* 'White [Horse] Owners Society' among the Hunkpapas.

[11]The meaning of the words "Icis" and "Wacandi" is not fully understood. According to White Bull, the Northern Hunkpapas consisted of four bands: the Bad Bow Band under Sitting Bull, the Sore Back Band under Red Horn, the Meat Necklace Band under Gall, and the Holy Band under Long Horn. The Holy Band, or *Wakan* Band, is probably the Wacandi Band. The word 'Icis' probably identified the *Icira* Band, which joined the Bad Bow Band and accepted Sitting Bull as their chief.

300, [totalling] 2300 lodges in all. About one to three men in each lodge. More than half [the population] in camp could fight. Little less than 2300 warriors in camp.

Cheyennes and Oglalas were camping south and east [in valley]. Custer could only see Hunkpapas, Minneconjous, and Sans Arc.[12]

Minneconjou chiefs: Makes Room[13] (my father), Flying By,[14] Black Shield,[15] Lame Deer,[16] [and] Black Moon (not same as Hunkpapa). Sans Arc chiefs: Two Eagle, His High Horse, Black Eagle,[17] [and] Blue Coat. [I] don't know [names of] Cheyenne chiefs. Oglalas: Sweat, Red Cloud not there, [but] Young Red Cloud[18] was there.

[I] didn't go to Sitting Bull's camp these three days [prior to June 25].

When did they hear soldiers were coming?

Two scouts returned [with news that] a man and son [had] gone out and son [was] killed.[19] News came in before noon, [about] 10 o'clock. White Bull [was] out with bunch of horses on north side of river, not over a quarter mile away, when

---

[12]That is, Custer could only see the southern end of the village when he and his troops gained the heights near Reno Hill.

[13]Makes Room, or rather They Make Room for Him *Kiyukanpi* (1825–1905), was a Minneconjou Scalp Shirt Wearer and the father of White Bull and One Bull. Makes Room was married to Pretty Feather Woman, the younger sister of Sitting Bull.

[14]Flying By was a Scalp Shirt Wearer and was the principal Minneconjou chief during the Wagon Box Fight of 1867. He did not have any children and should not be confused with the Minneconjou of like name who was the son of Chief Lone Horn.

[15]Black Shield was a Scalp Shirt Wearer and led the Minneconjous during the Phil Kearney Fight of 1866. He had a son named Big Crow.

[16]Lame Deer was a Minneconjou Scalp Shirt Wearer. He was killed on Lame Deer Creek, Montana, on May 5, 1877, by troops under Gen. Nelson A. Miles.

[17]Black Eagle was a Minneconjou Scalp Shirt Wearer. He was appointed to this position because of his likable character and gentle disposition. He surrendered to Miles in October 1876.

[18]Born in 1855, Jack Red Cloud was the son of Old Red Cloud, the leader of the Oglala Bad Face Band. Jack Red Cloud left the agency in April 1876 with the Black Elk Band and subsequently participated in the Rosebud Fight of June 17. His conduct during this engagement was judged to be less than exemplary according to his fellow tribesmen.

[19]This is a reference to the killing of Deeds. His father, Little Bear, escaped.

news came. [He] knew of news [that] one [was] killed. [He was] then [on] long flat and he could see soldiers [coming] from south first. He took horses in when he saw them.

I caught and got on my war horse and went to Sitting Bull's camp, and everyone got on their horses to be ready. When I got to Sitting Bull's camp his wife, child and everyone ran away, and every man who could fight got on a horse and stood [his] ground. Sitting Bull [was] with [the] latter and had [a] gun. ([He had a] 44 [caliber] Winchester rifle and 45 [caliber] pistol [which] White Bull had given both to him.[20])

[What was] Sitting Bull's dress?

Rush doings and no special dress, just shirt and leggings [that] he already had [on]. No feathers, [and] riding a black horse.[21] Sitting Bull said, "Brave up, boys, it will be a hard time, brave up." Pizi[22] [was] in camp, but I didn't see him at that time. Four Horns [was] there on a mixed roan and bay horse, and had bow and arrows.

Had soldiers stopped coming?

Indians and soldiers had started firing when White Bull arrived. Doesn't know if Sitting Bull shot [his gun]. [An] old man [named] Three Bears[23] [was] wounded at standstill-shooting. Some [were] on horse[back] and some on foot. Ground unlevel between Indians and soldiers. Indians [were] in sort of [a] draw, or valley. [There] was timber along [the] river. Soldiers [were] shooting north.

---

[20]This weapon, or one similar given to Sitting Bull by Johnny Brughiere in October of 1876, was confiscated by Major David S. Brotherton at the formal surrender on July 20, 1881. It was described as a 44-caliber Winchester carbine, Model 1866, which was donated to the Smithsonian in 1946 by one of Brotherton's heirs.

[21]According to One Bull, Sitting Bull rode a black horse with white fetlocks and a white blaze in the face. Sitting Bull was dressed in buckskin garments, the shirt having been ornamented with green quills and human hair which hang from the sleeves. He wore a single eagle feather upright at the back of the head and his face was unpainted.

[22]*Pizi* 'Gall' (1840–1893) was the leader of the Meat Necklace Band.

[23]Three Bears was an elderly Hunkpapa who was mortally wounded during the valley fight. He died on June 29 on Wood Louse Creek, at the foot of the Big Horn Mountains.

[Did you see] Indian scouts with [the] soldiers?

Too big a hurry, [I] didn't look. White Bull [was] near [the] river, and Oglalas and Cheyennes back. Sitting Bull [was] near [the] river and [was] with White Bull. White Bull started in one place with Sitting Bull; [but] then they move around and White Bull loses track of Sitting Bull. White Bull [was] not standing around looking, but [was] shooting.

Before the soldiers go back to [the] timber, young Sioux [named] Dog with Horns gets shot.[24] [While] the soldiers retreated to timber, Good Bear Boy gets shot in hip, and Lone Bull saves him. Then [the] soldiers reach [the] timber and untie [their] horses and run across [the] river. But before [the] soldiers get across [the] stream they kill Swift Bear [and] kill White Bull (no relative of White Bull), and wound Chased by Owl.[25]

Indians follow across [the] river and are close enough to strike soldiers, but he doesn't remember [the name of] anyone striking soldiers. He didn't [strike any]. He was shooting and didn't see Sitting Bull. Didn't look for him. Some soldiers and some Indians killed across the river, and as White Bull couldn't catch up, he stopped. The braves crossed the stream and White Bull also crossed. [The] stream [was] not deep enough to swim; pretty wide, but not deep.

After soldiers [stopped] on hill, a bunch of Indians stopped on side of hill, and White Bull stopped there. Sitting Bull [was] not in this bunch. Didn't see Sitting Bull cross [the] stream.

[From] where we were standing on side of hill we saw another troop moving from [the] east toward [the] north, [to] where [the fleeing] camp was moving, and we charged; it

---

[24]Dog with Horns was a young Minneconjou who was killed early in the valley fight. His body was found by his brother, Feather Earring.

[25]White Bull and Swift Bear were the brothers of the Hunkpapa, Crow King. Chased by Owls was a Two Kettle Lakota. These men were all slain on the west side of the river.

was Custer. We went down [the] east side of [the] river and we rode straight to Custer. [It] was three miles from where we left Reno to Custer.

[We] chased Custer [an] indefinite distance. Couldn't see Custer as he was [among the soldiers] in [the] companies. But [it] was about [a] mile from Custer to hill, [and soldiers] still riding in walking-trotting [gait], still close together. Custer didn't stop before they reached [the hill?]; they kept shooting as Custer kept moving.

[There were] many little bunches of Indians, [but] White Bull doesn't know total number of Indians. Pizi stayed in camp now. Sitting Bull must have gone back. With White Bull going to Custer [were] Iron Lightning, Owns the Horn, Shoots Bear as He Runs,[26] [and] two Cheyennes. White Bull [had] crossed river at south side of Hunkpapas [and] stayed across [while] going to Custer.

Some Indians went up [a] draw [Deep Coulee?] to Custer, White Bull with them, [along with] a lot of them. When up in [the] draw, Custer saw them and took shots at them, so they moved back south a [little] ways. Custer [soldiers were] at standstill and got off horses to shoot, [and] then got back on [again]. [They] made four companies and one company was shooting at them in the draw. [He] doesn't know color of horses in [last] company.

On with the battle! After they shoot us back, I left my bunch [and] worked [my way] around to the east and threw in with another [bunch], and now many bunches [were] on south [side]. We took charge at one company and drove them back to where [the present] Custer monument is. There was much dust, and we rode among them and pulled them from their horses.

War started about 9 or 10 [o'clock] and lasted till about

---

[26]Shoots the Bear as He Runs was a Minneconjou. He was killed by Crows in 1879 during a Sioux horse-stealing expedition near the Powder River.

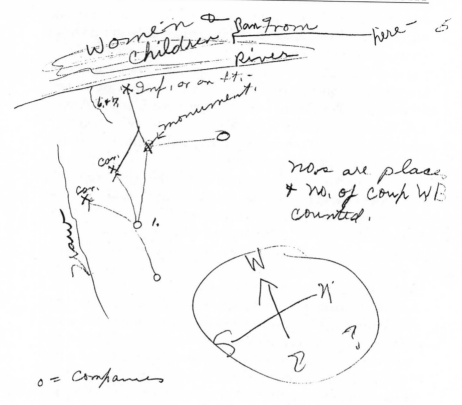

o = Companies

noon. [I] never saw Sitting Bull in [the] whole fight. Sitting Bull never told White Bull about his part in [the] fight. Some chiefs told women and children [that] fight would not last long and [that they] need not run [any] farther. Some chiefs and braves stayed with women and children.

Didn't know who white general was; didn't see him. Soldiers [were] not very good fighters and most were drunk and scared when [they] saw so many Indians. I didn't know of whiskey [found] on soldiers, nor [did I] smell it afterwards.

Were [soldier] horses used up?

Not fast, [but I] didn't notice if tired.

White Bull got one sorrel, a good horse; this was not

Custer's. [It] had saddlebags on it [and] shells and bullets in saddlebags. [I also] got a good gun [which] had no trouble with cartridges sticking. Had gun been fired when he got it? Yes, all empty [and] not many cartridges [found] around soldiers. [We] got some pistols that hadn't been used. [Also] many cartridge belts, and few [of these] had been used.

[We] charged soldiers at close hand. Some soldiers ran. Others shot with pistol, and others shot with rifle. Some beat with rifle as [a] club.

White Bull got seven coups. Coup counts if horse hits man. . . .[27]

Where monument [now] stands another Indian showed White Bull Custer's body. Clothes had been taken away, and Custer was lying naked. Bad Juice [aka Bad Soup] shown White Bull Custer's body. This Indian often was with soldiers. Later White Bull was watering horses and [noticed] an Indian [who] had [a] sorrel horse. White Bull said, "Is that a good horse?" The Indian said, "I know it is a good horse as it was Long Hair's." Sounds the Ground as He Walks had Custer's horse, a Santee, son of Inkpaluta.

White Bull had never see Custer before; neither other Hunkpapas, nor Sitting Bull, I think. [Did] Sitting Bull go to battlefield after [the] fight? Don't know.

About three days after [the] war I saw Sitting Bull in White Mountains where camp had been moved. They saw Three Stars [Gen. George Crook] go south from N [north?] at this time, and some Indians chased [him], but Sitting Bull never mentioned Custer again.

[The] teamsters and [a] few others [who] they had chased up [Reno] hill were still there. We had a little fight with them that afternoon and late night, and next morning. I [then] took a little nap, and while I [was] asleep, another bunch of soldiers came from [the] north. Three of us went to look for

---

[27]Excluded from the transcript is a description of White Bull's coups which was appended to his earlier account published in *Lakota Recollections*.

them. We saw them and returned to camp, and as they were moving camp to White Mountains, we were two days behind on the moving, and it was three days later [when] we caught up with [the] camp on Powder River in White Mountains. Here I first saw Sitting Bull.

[The] camp [had] followed upriver from Custer battle to Big Horns (White Mountains). Took three days to move camp. Everyone who had been in Custer battle was at White Mountains. Next we ([the] whole works) followed back [on] our tracks, past Custer field to Rosebud. From there [we] came north to Tongue River; then down Tongue River to mouth [and] cut over east to Powder River; then on east, [the] whole shebang still together. [We] camped on branch of Powder River; then went east to Beaver Creek, [and] then on to Little Missouri River. Here they split. Some went to Slim Butte and had [a] fight.[28]

[He] doesn't know [how much] time [it took to move] from [the] Custer fight to [the] Little Missouri. (Probably June to July, or August.) Sitting Bull spent that winter on [the] Yellowstone. Sitting Bull had fight here with Bear Coat.[29]

Before above [fight took place], Sitting Bull attacked a wagon train.[30] [Was] White Bull present? Yes. The Indians tried to go to [a] bunch of wagons, but [the] infantry shot at [the] Indians and kept firing, and White Bull got shot in left

---

[28]The battle of Slim Buttes, South Dakota, took place on September 9, 1876, when units from the Fifth Cavalry under Capt. Anson Mills captured a Minneconjou village of thirty-seven lodges with all their contents. The Indians managed to escape with a loss of five killed and a dozen captured.

[29]This was the aforementioned fight with General Miles on Cedar Creek, Montana, October 21, 1876.

[30]The *Record of Engagements* states: On October 10, [1876,] Capt. C. W. Miner, Twenty-Second Infantry, with Companies H, G, and K, escorting a train of ninety-four wagons, started from the camp at mouth of Glendive Creek, Montana, for the cantonment at mouth of Tongue River. The train was attacked in its camp that night by Indians estimated at from four to six hundred, and forty-seven mules stampeded and [were] captured. In this crippled condition the train attempted to reach Clear Creek, eight miles farther on, being constantly harassed by the hostiles in large force, but finding it impossible to continue, returned to Glendive Creek for re-enforcements.

arm above [the] elbow, breaking [the] bone. White Bull didn't fall off [his pony], but when [going back] to his village and [while] almost home, he nearly fell, and small boys came and helped him three or four miles to [the] camp. . . .

[There were] no whites in Sitting Bull's camp at the Little Bighorn. No soldiers killed themselves. [There were] no captives.

The teamsters having become too demoralized to proceed, forty-one of them were discharged and soldiers were detailed to drive [the wagons]. The escort, now consisting of five companies of infantry, numbering eleven officers and 185 men, under command of Lieut. Col. E. S. Otis, Twenty-Second Infantry, again attempted to carry these much-needed supplies to the garrison at Tongue River.

October 15, on Spring Creek, the Indians, increased to an estimated strength of from seven to eight hundred warriors, again attacked the train, which, however, formed in compact lines, pressed on, the infantry escort charging the Indians repeatedly and driving them back, while the wagons slowly advanced. Three or four scouts from Colonel Miles' command were met here, having been attacked by Indians and one of their party killed. The train proceeded, with the escort skirmishing, until Clear Creek was reached, the point from which Captain Miner had previously been obliged to return. Here the Indians made the most determined attack, firing the prairie, and the wagons being obliged to advance through the flames. Compactly arranged in four lines, the wagons proceeded, the entire escort being engaged in alternately charging the Indians, driving them back, and then regaining the moving teams; three or four of the escort were wounded and a considerable number of Indian saddles emptied.

On October 16, whilst advancing, an Indian runner approached and left upon a hill the following communication: "Yellowstone [River]. I want to know what you are doing traveling on this road. You scare all the buffalo away. I want to hunt in this place. I want you to turn back from here. If you don't I will fight you again. I want you to leave what you have got here and turn back from here. I am your friend, Sitting Bull. [P.S.] I mean all the rations you have and some powder. Wish you would write as soon as you can."

Colonel Otis sent out a scout, named Jackson, with a reply to Sitting Bull's note, stating that he intended to take the train through to Tongue River, and would be pleased to accommodate the Indians with a fight any time.

The train proceeded, the Indians surrounding it, and keeping up firing at long range. After proceeding a short distance, two Indians appeared with a flag of truce, and communication was again opened with the hostiles, who stated they were hungry, tired of war, and wanted to make peace. Sitting Bull wanted to meet Colonel Otis outside of the lines of the escort, which invitation, however, Colonel Otis declined, though professing a willingness to meet Sitting Bull inside the lines of his troops. This the wary savage was afraid to do, but sent three chiefs to represent him. Colonel Otis made them a present of 150 pounds of hard bread and two sides of bacon, said that he had no authority to treat with them, but that the Indians could go to Tongue River, and there make known their wishes regarding surrender. The train moved on, and the Indians fell to its rear, finally disappearing altogether.

Indians killed in Custer Battle:

1. Three Bear
2. Dog with Horn
3. Chased by Owl
4. White Eagle
5. Swift Bear
6. White Bull
7. Standing Elk
8. Bear with Horn
9. Lone Dog
10. Elk Bear
11. Cloud Man
12. Hawk Man
13. Kill Him
14. Guts
15. Plenty Lice
16. Red Face
17. Bad Light Hair
18. Young Skunk
19. Back Bone of Dog
20. Left Handed Ice
21. Owns Red Horse
22. Young Bear
23. Flying By
24. Mustache
25. Black Fox
26. Swift Cloud
27. Long Robe [Long Road]
28. Business [aka] Deeds (Wicohan), the first one to be shot

[Were any] Indians killed with arrows?

Don't know. [There were] some Ree scouts with Custer. [Statements] all wrong that Indians killed [own] Indians,[31] or [that] soldiers kill soldiers by mistake. All [fighting took place] in daylight.

[The] night after fight White Bull [was] around wagons [on Reno Hill], but nothing doing in camp. Victory dance [took place] four days later near White Mountains.

[Were] any Indians buried in tent around [a] drum?

No such thing. Too many tongues; many lies.[32]

---

[31]Despite White Bull's assertion, it is a fact that several Indians were killed accidentally by their own allies. It is known that the Arapaho, Left Hand, lanced a Hunkpapa in the mistaken belief that his victim was an enemy scout. A similar error may have caused the death of the Cheyenne, Lame White Man. According to his tribesman Yellow Nose, Lame White Man was shot to death because he was wearing a blue jacket taken from a dead soldier, and he was subsequently scalped by Little Crow, the brother of Chief Hump. It is also known that Noise Walking, the son of the Cheyenne shaman White Bull, was stabbed a number of times by a hasty Sioux who mistook the Cheyenne boy for an enemy. Lastly, a number of Indian accounts mention that some of their casualties were caused by stray arrows.

When soldiers first came [did] Sitting Bull take one twin and ride away?[33]

Must be so as Sitting Bull and I were there. Then I left and didn't see Sitting Bull again.

Ever know Sitting Bull to be [a] coward?

No.

Was Sitting Bull on hill making medicine during battle?

No, just talk. Sitting Bull [was] shot through foot and was not healing right, so Sitting Bull couldn't run. No reason for Sitting Bull not [to be] in fight. If not, [he] was taking women and children back, [and] then went to fight. One Bull may know [more].

Why didn't [the] Indians kill [the] men on [Reno] hill?

[The Indians] talked among themselves and [decided] that [it] was enough, but hung around teamsters, thinking maybe more soldiers would come. Teamsters dug holes so deep Indians could hardly see them.

Sitting Bull fought some [soldiers] after Custer. [He] would fight if they came to him, but would not go and start fights. He didn't want to fight, but would if some one came to him to fight. If Sitting Bull didn't fight Custer [it was] not because he couldn't.

Some say chief didn't fight?

Yes, generally chiefs say not to fight unless enemy came around and bothered women and children. Then [chiefs] encourage boys to fight. Women and children [were] afraid of soldiers as [they] didn't want to be shot down. . . .

Winter before Custer battle [Hunkpapas camped at] mouth of Powder River; [this was] Sitting Bull's band. White Bull

---

[32]This statement is in reference to the discovery of several dead Lakotas whose bodies were ceremonially arranged around a drum near the middle of the deserted Indian village.

[33]E. H. Allison learned from his Hunkpapa relatives that Sitting Bull's wife was so frightened by Reno's attack that she accidentally left one of the twin infants behind in the lodge. She later realized her mistake and went back to get him. The one left behind was nicknamed *Ihpeya Nanpapi* 'Abandoned One,' while the other twin was called *Yuha Nanpapi* 'Fled With.'

[camped] at mouth of Tongue River with Minneconjous and Sans Arc. Crazy Horse [camped] around White Mountain.

Runners from [the] Agency did not come to tell them to come to [the] Agency. [There were] travelers, but no runners with message. That winter [was] a very bad winter with much snow, and [it] would take 20 days to move camp to Agency. But if [travel] was [with an] automobile they might make it. [We used] calf-high moccasins lined with buffalo wool, but no snow shoes.

Could Reno have saved himself in the timber?

Yes. It was foolish to run across the river.

[Does] Walter's [Campbell] story agree with White Bull?

White Bull didn't know about soldiers and their orders. Walter [should] write about them [soldiers] coming and their actions. It must be two days after the fight that soldiers come and see the dead of Custer.

Reno hit camp about 10:30. Horses [were] all out on prairie. [It was] known that soldiers would come that day. Scouts saw them coming at Sun Dance ground; three or four scouts, one [of whom] is Owns Bob Tail Horse. Scouts saw soldiers coming three days before. Scouts brought word three days before soldiers came, and everyday [they] reported again. [A] crier announced that soldiers were coming three days before, [first] in the P.M., [then] late at night, [and] repeat [it again] next morning. Warrior society through lodges of "soldiers" gave out [the] news. Name of crier? [Name not recorded.] [Crier] announced every day. Words of [the] crier about noon [on] day before, [were:] "The soldiers will be here tomorrow. Be ready."[34]

Did any Indians wish to pull out?

No, all stick together.

Did they know how many soldiers [were] coming?

No.

---

[34]A similar announcement was made by the Cheyenne prophet Old Brave Wolf.

Did they know what soldier chief was coming?

No, not acquainted. Very few Indians knew Custer. [We] did not know who was coming.

Did they dance war dances?

No, [only] social dances.

[It is] true that many Agency Indians came out to hunt [and] not to fight. . . .

White Bull had 20 horses at [the] Little Bighorn. Sitting Bull had more than 20 at Little Bighorn. [The] richest Indian had 40 to 60 horses at Little Bighorn. Wounded Hand had most among Minneconjous, about 100 head.

Habits of Horses: Picketed gentle horses all night; [at] daybreak turn loose, water, graze till noon, water at noon, graze [all] afternoon, water in evening, and picketed at night.

White Bull and horses [at] Little Bighorn: Took 'em out, went back to eat and return[ed], stay half an hour, [but] no time to water [because] war started.

[What do you think of the] white men's way of fighting?

They don't know how to fight. [I] saw lots of them.

[What are their] mistakes?

[They] should act more lively, like Indians, but [they get] too many orders and don't try to save themselves; they stand up straight and run straight. [It is] easy to shoot them. Half [of them] obey orders, and half don't. (Deploying he means?)

[Would you] rather fight white soldiers or Crow Indians?

Either [of them] is just shooting, but in hand to hand fights, Crows [are] worse.

Different ways to fight: 500 yards in daytime and get Crow horses. Then Crows run after them. If they start early, enough [Sioux] will get the horses home. Ordinarily Crows come at night. [Crows came only] once in daytime when White Bull [was] little; but all Crows [were] killed before they got home. Indian fights [are] more lively than [fights] with whites.

Never fought with Ree. [The] people around [the] agency did most [of the] fighting [with the] Ree. [These were the] Yanktons. Rees [fought] about like Crows. Shoshones [fought] better than Crows.

[Did] White Bull fight others besides Crows?

Flatheads about [the] same as Crows. [They] fire from long range; then, when [they] turn around, [they] sure run. All tribes they fought with had more guns than Sioux.

Never knew of soldiers selling guns to Sioux. Did know of traders selling guns to Sioux. Also, during fight with white soldiers at Fort Bennet [traders] sold many [guns] to any Indian who had [goods to pay] price, in Agency or out[side].

[Were any] traders upriver with guns on boats to sell?

Didn't hear of it.

[Did] Indians have plenty [of] powder and bullets while fighting whites?

Early in spring [Indian] people from [the] west come to agency to trade buffalo hides for powder and ball. Next time [they come] in fall. Sitting Bull did this at Fort Peck when White Bull [was] with him about five years before Custer fight, [about] 1869–1870.

[A] commissioner [came] to [the] Indians four years before [the] Custer fight, and Sitting Bull's brother-in-law [Covers His Head] went to Fort Peck to talk to commissioner. [Sitting Bull] had three brother-in-laws at that time: Makes Room [or] Kiyukanpi, [who was] White Bull's father, Covers His Head [or] Pamahe Techauke, [and] His Horse Looking or Tasunka Wakita. . . .

12TH FIGHT: TEAMSTER PART OF CUSTER FIGHT

After Custer Battle some [whites] run back and get on [Reno] hill,[35] and warriors run after [them] (south and northeast side). White Bull on northeast [with] bunch, [and]

---

[35]This statement probably refers to the withdrawal of troops from Weir Point to Reno Hill.

Sitting Bull on south [with] bunch. Warriors [were] chasing retreating soldiers. White Bull quits a ways from soldiers, and south bunch [was a] little nearer [to] soldiers.

[In] White Bull's bunch [was] Backbone of a Dog [who] was shot in [the] head and killed by soldiers.

Sitting Bull's bunch [saw] two soldiers separate [from rest] and they kill the soldiers and run out and count coup. Shell Earring and Snake Creek run out.[36]

After [that] both bunches of Indians started for whole bunch of soldiers and chase them out of their holes and Long Robe [*sic*] gets shot.[37]

That night Indians surrounded place [on hill] and fired [shots], but don't know whether anyone there [was] killed. Next morning we hang around till noon, and are [getting] hungry and thirsty, as most Indians are.

I came home [from Reno Hill] and got my lunch and [took a] nap, and by this time Benteen [Gen. Gibbon and Montana Column] was coming on north side of camp. So I took two boys, and myself makes three, and we went down to where they stopped, and I got seven cavalry horses. By this time the bunch of Indians were starting [to retreat], and I got my horses and went through [the vacated] Indian camp.

About [the] middle of (3rd) night we were camping toward White Mountains. Sitting Bull not in fight versus Gibbon.

What time [did] White Bull take nap?

[At] noon, day after Custer was killed. Was at home half an hour; then [came] disturbance that Benteen [Gibbon] was coming from north of Reno.

[Were there any] wagons with Benteen [Gibbon]?

------

[36]This is perhaps a reference to the killing of two unknown soldiers who failed in their attempt to get water from the river. However, none of the survivors mention the killing of any of the water carriers, of whom fifteen earned the coveted Medal of Honor.

[37]*Canku Hanska* 'Long Road' was a young Sans Arc who was killed June 26 on the south side of Reno Hill, some seventy feet from H Company's line. It was learned from his grieving parents that he had grown despondent by the death of his older brother, slain in the Rosebud Fight, and apparently did not want to live any longer.

Don't know.

[Any] cavalry?

Don't know.

[What] time did camps pull out?

Still on [flat] when I left to go to Benteen [Gibbon]. [It took] about 20 miles to [ride] north to Benteen.

[What] time [did you] get back with [captured] horses?

Sundown.

[Had] camp already moved out of sight?

Yes.

[Were] any soldiers with Reno now?

[They were] out of sight and [I] couldn't see [them], but warriors [were] gathering as he returned from Benteen [Gibbon]. White Bull told them [the size] of Benteen's troops. They told him camp was moved, and he didn't stop [very long].

Camp [was] scared because more soldiers came from [the] north. White Bull feels every man must protect himself, but it wasn't right to kill all [of] them. Sitting Bull said, "I feel sorry that too many [have been] killed on each side; but when Indians must fight, they must."

I jerked a soldier off his horse, and after he fell Crazy Horse counted the second coup, and he later charged through all [of] them. Crazy Horse wore no feather, [and wore] loose hair, ordinary hair, [and painted his] face spotted. [He] carried [a] gun. Crazy Horse counted second coup on White Bull's coup number two. Crazy Horse [then] ran through infantry, after coup count, and [was] followed by White Bull, [charging] from north toward west.[38] Cheyennes and all Indians [were] mixed, so [I] couldn't tell who fought where. White Bull didn't see Pizi.

Did Sitting Bull tell Indians to go away and let soldiers go?

Didn't hear [that]; no time to talk.

---

[38]This action took place on the east side of Custer Ridge where Crazy Horse charged through Keogh's line and through a gap in Custer Ridge which brought him onto the west slope. This gap was filled in 1934 to facilitate the present blacktop.

The Shoots Walking Statement

Editorial note: The Shoots Walking statement is contained in the Walter Stanley Campbell Collection, Box III, Western History Collections, University of Oklahoma. It is reproduced hereafter with their permission. A subject search failed to disclose any information on this Hunkpapa eyewitness.

_____

[Standing Rock Reservation]
[ca. 1935]

WAUKUTEMONIE'S STORY OF CUSTER'S LAST STAND

(Waukutemonie [Shoots Walking] was about the age of 16 at the time of the battle.)

Long Elk, Pretty Bear and Elk Heart were the first three that were wounded [during Reno's attack], and then the Indians began to fight.

I was but a young boy and wanted to go with the men to fight, and my mother and sister came and put their arms about me and begged me not to go for fear I would be killed. After I got on my horse they held me back, so that when the first battle occurred I did not get through. Just before that

[time] there had been some of the Crows fighting, and Custer [Crook] had fought with them, and two or three [Lakota] men were killed. That was the reason my mother and sister did not want me to go.

I finally broke away and came down there, but did not go where Reno was. The younger fellows were wild about the fighting and all went over the bluff, but it was only a few moments before everybody came. We did not have much time for preparation or anything else, and [we] struck with the butts of our whips.

Did Custer's men send their horses back and fight without them?

A great many left their horses behind and some fought from them.

Did the smoke and dust get so thick that one could not see?

Most of the soldiers acted as though they were drunk. Many of them threw their guns down, and at no time was there [so] much shooting that one could not see.[1]

How long was it from the time Custer came through the hill till all were wiped out?

It was a very little while for when they began to kill they dropped as fast as they could.

Could Reno have gotten through to help Custer?

Reno could not have reached Custer at all; the entrenchments were too far away.

The young Indian boys all wanted to go on and fight the rest of the way, but the older Indians would not let them; they told us that if this many white soldiers had come, that without doubt there were many more on farther, and it would be too dangerous with no prospect of winning. Scouts advised the Indians after looking through their glasses [at

---

[1]However, according to Little Soldier and One Bull, the discharge of black powder darkened the battlefield to such extent that the flashes of rifle fire could be seen.

Gibbon's column] that they better let Reno go and take care of themselves.

After this battle our family went with other families to the White Mountains (Rocky Mountains [Big Horn Mountains]), and then turned and came back to the Rosebud again, and then to the Little Missouri, thence to the Thick Woods river also. When they got to the Thick Woods river twenty families came back and two went to Canada. Our family was with those who came back. . . .

Waukutemonie said further: "I killed two men who had guns in their hands, and I killed them with my revolver. They did not know enough to shoot. They had rifles and were near me too. They did not fire their guns together and they fought without system whatsoever."

The Paul Noisy Statement

Editorial note: The Paul Noisy statement is housed in the Joseph G. Masters Collection, Box 2, Folder 15, "Explorations" 1936: Sioux and Cheyenne Accounts of the Custer Battle, Kansas State Historical Society. It is reproduced hereafter with their permission.

This statement which follows was obtained by Masters while en route to Fort Yates, North Dakota, to interview several elderly Hunkpapas. No data was located on the Brule authority.

Rosebud Indian Agency, South Dakota
July 25, 1936

[I] talked to Paul Noisy, a full-blood Sioux whose father was in the Custer Battle. [The] interpreter was Louis Roubidoux, or Roubideaux.[1] Paul Noisy says [the] Custer battle lasted about 2½ hours. [He] says [the] soldiers shot in nearly every direction. [He] says Crazy Horse was the real leader of the fight. Says it was [the] custom of [the] Indians to select someone to ride out in front of [the] Indians and in

---

[1]Louis Roubidoux was a mixed blood of French/Brule parentage. In his younger years he was employed as the official interpreter at the Brule Indian Agency and resided at the Jordan Trading Post.

front of [the] enemy. Crazy Horse was selected and was regarded as [the] real leader.[2] Foolish Elk corroborated this says Roubideaux (before Foolish Elk died).[3]

---

[2]The valor displayed by Crazy Horse on that occasion left a lasting impression on the Arapaho, Waterman, who vividly recalled that Crazy Horse was the bravest man he ever knew. He added that all the soldiers were shooting at Crazy Horse, but that none were able to hit him. This is confirmed by the Oglala Red Feather who stated that Crazy Horse rode between the opposing lines while blowing his eagle-bone whistle. This display of courage took place on the east side of Custer Ridge, near Keogh's location, where Crazy Horse later charged through a gap in Custer Ridge, splitting Keogh's battalion and causing its annihilation. The Oglala, He Dog, fondly remembered that everyone became brave when Crazy Horse appeared on the battlefield.

[3]Foolish Elk was a Brule Lakota. He sustained a gunshot wound during the Rosebud Fight and was convalescing in his lodge when Custer's troops appeared.

The Little Soldier Interview

Editorial note: The interview with Little Soldier is housed in the Joseph G. Masters Collection, Box 2, Folder 15, "Explorations" 1936: Sioux and Cheyenne Accounts of the Custer Battle, Kansas State Historical Society. It is reproduced hereafter with their permission.

Born about 1862, Little Soldier was the son of the Hunkpapa, Four Robes Woman, and the Yanktonai, Tall Soldier aka Holy Face Bear. Known to the whites as Henry Little Soldier, he became the stepson of Chief Sitting Bull as a result of his mother's remarriage in 1869. After the surrender, Little Soldier enlisted as an Indian Scout and was present during the killing of Sitting Bull. The interview which follows was arranged by Frank B. Zahn, agency interpreter, for which Little Soldier was compensated the sum of ten dollars.

Fort Yates, North Dakota
August 24, 1936

MORNING OF JUNE 25

I got up and went after [the] horses and [came] back to water [them]. I brought one horse back and kept him in camp. [I then] had breakfast, took bow and arrows and went down to [the] river to play with [the] boys. While we were there, I heard a camp crier riding along the camp on a swift horse, calling. We knew something must be up, so [we] came back to [the] tents and our people told us [that] two Indians already [had been] killed.

A young boy, Deeds, and Hona [were] shot at by soldiers. Both [were] shot at. Little Bear [was also] wounded, but got away. His horse was killed and he was shot in [the] leg. (Frank Zahn explains that when Little Bear's horse was shot and he was wounded so that he could not continue in the fight, that the Indians regarded and spoke of such a man as [being] dead. Little Bear was [the] father of Deeds and Hona and Mary Crawler.)[1]

The Battle Begins

We all looked east at [the] bluffs and saw three bodies of soldiers. [The] south body moved first and went south. Then the middle body [moved] and crossed. Everybody was running for horses. [I] saw Reno's men crossing the river. I saw two divisions of Reno's men coming, each carrying a flag. The soldiers who went north went behind the ridges. [They] rode bay and gray horses. I got on my horse and [so did] other warriors, and [Reno's] men shot into [the] Hunkpapa camp.

Hona is [a] brother of Deeds. [The] boy was over one mile from [the] camps when [he was] killed.[2]

---

[1]Little Bear was the leader of a Hunkpapa band. He was a celebrated warrior who was known for his ability to capture horses. He was the Camp Crier for the Silent Eaters Society and was described as giant in stature with a Mongolian face. He was instrumental in the release of Fanny Kelley, a white captive, in 1864. Little Bear, who may have been a Sans Arc by birth, is better known by the name *Slohan* 'Crawler,' and is sometimes identified by the colorful nickname of Brown Ass. He was killed by Indian Scouts during the arrest of Sitting Bull in 1890.

[2]*Hona* 'Little Voice' escaped unharmed. According to Minneconjou informants, Deeds was wounded by Reno's soldiers a short distance below the forks of Reno Creek, and died in the brush along the Little Bighorn. See also the map in the One Bull interview which identified Deed's kill site.

[The] women took [the] children. [The] older warriors were out hunting buffalo, [and] for that reason [only] boys [from] 13 to 18 [years old] did the fighting. Old men sang death songs for [the] warriors. Sweethearts, young Indian mothers, and children [were] all wailing and crying.

First the Indians rode to [the] soldiers holding horses and drove them away to cover. Then [the] warriors attacked the soldiers on foot. [These] soldiers lay down, and others got on [their] knees and others stood. Warriors rode into them.

[The] bullets came like hail when [the] fire first started. [The] bullets sounded like hail on [the] tepees and tree tops. [I] could see [the] bullets hit dirt. I was armed with my bow and arrows.

Indian horses were brought in and mounted by warriors

and squaws with hordes. Old decrepit men and women hurried on [and] walked ahead of squaws and children who rode behind them to protect them. Women would call to children, and children would recognize [their] mothers' voices.

As [the] warriors rode on, the soldiers ran and mounted any horse and stopped fighting. Hawk Man said, "Charge," and rode out in front at the soldiers alone the first time. So Hawk Man rode out in front and no [one] followed the first time. [The] second time [he] led.[3]

Where [the] soldiers plunged into [the] river it was like steep sides. Then from [the] east bank a body of soldiers [under Custer] charged down upon us. (There were other Indian camps up the river who did not know of the battle.) I saw Two Bull's horse killed in retreat. During all this time a single soldier came back who they killed.

[The] warriors followed Reno's men to [the] river, crossed [the] river and chased [the] soldiers clear up on top of [the] bluff. Before [the] Indians got to top we heard a commotion down the river, so we gave up the chase after Reno and turned back north and rode down the river.

CUSTER

Followed by clouds of dust, [the] soldiers showed themselves about —— [blank] miles away. Other Indians who were already downriver saw Custer's dust and crossed the river. Custer's men dismounted. [Their] horses got away and ran for [the] river. Custer's men were all scattered out. [The] soldiers lined up on a ridge; then they sang.[4] [The] Indians scared [the] horses [and] 100 [horses] were killed before [the] soldiers retreated on foot.[5] [The] horses got away and

---

[3]Hawk Man was a Hunkpapa Lakota. He was killed during the charge described above.

[4]The 'singing' heard by Little Soldier may have been military commands.

[5]This awful destruction of animals took place on Calhoun Ridge which was littered with horse bones until 1904.

ran to the river. [The] Indians were on [the] east side of [the] soldiers and all around them.

The soldiers wore campaign hats; coats light blue; and trousers of a lighter blue, with [a] yellow strip; yellow spears (guidons?) and horse towels. [The] soldiers wore black boots with flat heels and spurs with rowels.

None of Custer's soldiers got across the river to the west side of the Little Big Horn. [The discharge of] black powder made the whole battlefield dark and gray. It was so dark that we could see the flash of the rifles. No one knew it was Custer until afterwards. Some of Custer's men got into draws and coulees and fought there. From time to time Custer moved [his] flag from hill to hill. [The] Cheyennes and Sioux were soon all mixed-in together in the fight. [The] Indians took after a man who was running back. Lots of horses [were] wounded.

Did any of [the] soldiers kill themselves?

I think so.

[The] Indians plundered [the] soldiers. [The] Indians saw dozens of whiskey bottles on [the] ridge above the river. Some Indians could see soldiers a long ways away, passing the cup (whiskey). [The] Indians got [the] rifles of [the] soldiers as soon as they killed a soldier.

Down in Reno's fight [the] Indians [got] ammunition, and on Custer field grabbed [the] rifles. [The] Indians would not scalp soldiers with short hair. No glory to scalp anyone with short hair, [says] Frank Zahn.

[The] Indians surrounded Reno on the hill, and next morning fought again. The Indians left Reno Hill the second day around 2 or 3 P.M.

Custer part of fight lasted about an hour. Less than 1,000 warriors altogether fought against Custer. Sixty-four Indians were killed altogether on [the] battleground, and several died later.[6] [The] Indians captured or found 368 rifles. [The]

---

[6]Little Soldier told Walter Campbell in 1930 that the casualty count was fifty.

women and children used the cavalry saddles on [the] retreat after they left the camps for the southwest.

Little Soldier followed Sitting Bull to Canada. [Border between] Canada and U.S. is called "Line in Sacred Path." Earth mounds that [were] put up between [the] U.S. and Canada made a ditch, [which] resembles a ceremonial ditch that we had at [the] Sun Dance; hence, [we] called [the border] "Holy Path," or, "Sacred Line." [I] went to Canada fall of 1876.[7]

Great warriors: Crazy Horse was the greatest fighter, said Little Soldier. The greatest fighter in the whole battle was Crazy Horse. Little Soldier said that Sitting Bull, when breaking camp on the Rosebud where a group of young men were racing horses . . . [warned,] "You are racing your horses now, but don't race them too hard and play them out, for you all are going to have a big fight soon." [The] Indians think of Sitting Bull as a great seer [who was] respected at that time. Little Soldier's father was Long Soldier.

---

[7]Although it has generally been assumed that Sitting Bull's band did not cross into Canada until May of 1877, Little Soldier's statement contradicts this belief and suggests that the Hunkpapas moved across the border in 1876. This stay must have been of short duration because General Miles engaged the Hunkpapas near the Yellowstone in October of 1876. Little Soldier's recollection of the earlier date receives support from the Hunkpapa, White Hair on the Face, who recalled that Sitting Bull's band went *back* to Canada after having been fired upon by troops.

The One Bull Statement

Editorial note: The One Bull statement is housed in the Joseph G. Masters Collection, Box 2, Folder 15, "Explorations" 1936: Sioux and Cheyenne Accounts of the Custer Battle, Kansas State Historical Society. It is reproduced hereafter with their permission.

This statement was obtained by Masters through the services of Frank B. Zahn, agency interpreter. For information on One Bull, see his interview with Walter S. Campbell printed heretofore.

Fort Yates, North Dakota
August 24, 1936

Most of [the] warriors had —— [word omitted]. We did not ride our own horses. [We] seized the first one we could and mounted it and rode into battle. Many warriors [were only] 13 to 18 years [old]. Old men had gone out to hunt buffalo. We rode along the fleeing soldiers and clubbed them down. [The] Indians were shouting Hok-a-hey [Charge]. Black powder made [the] day dark so that flashes of rifle [fire] could be seen.

The Holy Face Bear Statement

Editorial note: The Holy Face Bear statement is housed in the Joseph G. Masters Collection, Box 2, Folder 15, "Explorations" 1936: Sioux and Cheyenne Accounts of the Custer Battle, Kansas State Historical Society. It is reproduced hereafter with their permission.

The statement which follows was obtained by Masters through the services of Frank B. Zahn, agency interpreter. A subject search failed to disclose any data on this Hunkpapa eyewitness. He may have been the father of Little Soldier.

Fort Yates, North Dakota
August 24, 1936

Holy Face Bear said that Sunday [June 25, 1876,] was a very hot and sultry day. Soldiers shot high over [the] heads of [the] Indians.[1] [Sitting Bull said,] "Wait, these men may want to make a treaty with us." We crossed the Greasy Grass while [going] after the soldiers. I never saw so many Indians in battle.

---

[1]Apparently the gun sights had not been adjusted. In addition, the Hunkpapa lodges were erected on the first bench of the flood plain, while the skirmish line stood on the second bench. Many of the Indian informants told of bullets rattling the tepee tops.

Hona was a brother of Deeds (who was ten years old).

Crawler [had] said, "We thought they were Holy Men." Later [he] said, "Remember the Washita."

Butler, who was trying to get through to Custer, shot many Indians. Every time he shot he brought down a warrior, said [the] Indians. [The] Indians respected him because he was so brave.[2]

The boy killed was Deeds. [The] first warrior killed was Hawk Man [a Hunkpapa].

---

[2]First Sgt. James Butler (1842–1876), member of L Company, was killed near Deep Coulee. He was described as a balding, heavyset man with side-whiskers. According to Gen. Godfrey, Butler's body contained several wounds and was partially stripped, scalped, and mutilated. A number of expended cartridges lay around the body. Butler's remains were exhumed in May of 1905 and were reinterred in the National Cemetery near Custer Hill.

The Little Voice Statement

Editorial note: The Little Voice statement is housed in the Joseph G. Masters Collection, Box 2, Folder 15, "Explorations" 1936: Sioux and Cheyenne accounts of the Custer Battle. It is reproduced hereafter with their permission.

Born about 1864, *Ho Na,* or *Ho la* 'Little Voice', was the son of the Hunkpapa band chief Crawler. The statement which follows was obtained by Masters through the services of Frank B. Zahn, agency interpreter.

Fort Yates, North Dakota
August 24, 1936

Bloody Knife was killed. Bob Tail Bull (Ree) [was killed] by Bobtail Bull, a Hunkpapa.[1] Isaiah [was] killed by His Holy Pipe.[2] I heard [that a] Santee [named] Gray Earth

---

[1]Born about 1831, the Arickara, Bobtail Bull, was the Pipe Bearer (leader) of the Ree Scouts. He held the enlisted rank of sergeant and was killed on the east side of the river during the retreat. His brother was the Cheyenne, Plenty Crows, who was taken captive as a young boy by the Cheyenne and was raised as one of their own.

The Hunkpapa, Bobtail Bull, was a soldier of the Fox Warrior Society and member of Sitting Bull's bodyguard. He surrendered in 1881 and enlisted with the Standing Rock Indian Police and was present during the killing of Sitting Bull.

[2]After being mortally wounded by the Hunkpapa, His Holy Pipe, Isaiah Dorman was shot to death at close range by the Hunkpapa, Eagle Robe Woman, in revenge for the slaying of a relative.

Track killed Custer.[3] [In the] Reno Fight, [the] Indians rode among the soldiers and clubbed them. Crawler shouted, "Remember the Washita." Rain in the Face said [that during the] greatest fighting [the] Indians shouted, "There was never a better day to die." In less than 40 minutes the fight with Reno was over.

Brother of Rain in the Face says that Rain in the Face did not cut out [the] heart of Tom Custer. [The] excitement was so great that no one knew Tom Custer or General Custer. Hona [was the] brother of Deeds.

---

[3]Gray Earth Track was a Santee who sought sanctuary in Canada with Sitting Bull. According to the Hunkpapa Good Voiced Dog, Gray Earth Track captured a sorrel with white fetlocks and a blaze in the face, along with a military saddle, bridle, and other equipment, including two white-handled pistols. Gray Earth Track also possessed a watch and papers which he had taken from the body of a soldier wearing a fringed buckskin jacket.

The Mary Crawler Statement

Editorial note: The Mary Crawler statement is housed in the Joseph G. Masters Collection, Box 2, Folder 15, "Explorations" 1936: Sioux and Cheyenne Accounts of the Custer Battle, Kansas State Historical Society. It is reproduced hereafter with their permission.

Born about 1854, *Tashna Mani* 'Moving Robe Woman,' was the daughter of the Hunkpapa band chief Crawler. On the Standing Rock Agency rolls, Moving Robe was listed under her father's name, and having been given a Christian first name, she became known to the whites as Mary Crawler. The statement which follows was obtained by Masters through the services of Frank B. Zahn, agency interpreter. For her full account of the Custer battle, see Moving Robe's interview in Hardorff, *Lakota Recollections of the Custer Fight,* pp. 91–96.

Fort Yates, North Dakota
August 24, 1936

Mary Crawler, [an] Indian woman who fought Custer, was [the] daughter of Crawler and [the] sister of Deeds (boy

10 yrs old [and] first [one] killed), and when [she] heard that her brother was killed she rushed into [the] battle.

An Indian rode past our camp and shouted, "Make ready, the soldiers are coming!" It was hard to hold our horses back for they were all excited with the shooting and running. I had a Colt revolver and shot at several soldiers.[1]

[In the] Custer Fight some of [the] dead soldiers still had [their] trigger fingers (swelled) in [the] trigger guard of [their] revolvers. I washed the dirt from Custer's face to tell who he was. Custer's men got to the river above the beaver dam where the water was very deep. [The] soldiers dismounted and fired. [The] soldiers' horses got loose and ran to the river. Their packs got loose and floated down the river. ([The] horses wanted water.) [The] packs [were] fished out by [the] squaws. [The] mules' packs got loose.

[The] soldiers got down to the river (at Medicine Tail Creek), but did not cross. Custer did not know where to cross. [The] Indians crossed below the beaver dam. Long before Custer got to the river Custer began shooting to try to scare the Indians.

[The] Indians would have cut Custer to pieces had they known him. They did not respect him. They regarded him as untrue to his own word for he had said he would not fight [Indians] any more.[2]

---

[1]Mary Crawler killed two of Custer's troopers—shooting one soldier and hacking the other one to death with her sheath knife.

[2]This statement, only partially correct, has reference to a curse placed upon Custer in March of 1869 by the Southern Cheyenne leader Medicine Arrows. After smoking the pipe, Medicine Arrows had said to Custer, "If you are acting treachery towards us, sometime you and your whole command will be killed." After the pipe ritual was completed, Medicine Arrows poured the ashes from the bowl over the toes of Custer's boots to bring him bad luck.

The Eagle Bear Interview

Editorial note: The Eagle Bear interview is contained in a field despatch forwarded from Pine Ridge on September 25, to an unidentified newspaper, of which a clipping is in the author's collection. A subject search failed to locate any information on this Oglala eyewitness.

Pine Ridge, South Dakota
September 25 [1936]

[Eagle Bear] was standing under a crudely-built sun shelter in front of his one-room log cabin where he lives with his brother, Fool's Crow.[1] Eagle Bear's long, gray hair, parted in the middle, hung in two braids down his back. He wore an old pair of corduroy trousers, a faded blue shirt and shabby moccasins. A blue bandanna handkerchief was tied around his neck. . . .

"Eagle Bear, how did the battle with Custer begin?" the woman interpreter, Josephine, put the question to the Indian. The word "battle" was used judiciously because old-time Indians dislike the word "massacre" in describing Custer's defeat. The Indian looked stolidly at the ground, then grunt-

---

[1]Possibly Frank Fool's Crow, an Oglala Holy Man.

ed a few words. "He says the fight happened so long ago he must think awhile," Josephine said. . . .

"Custer was the blame for the battle," Eagle Bear said, speaking slowly. "Our people wanted peace. We did not want to fight the white men anymore. If Custer had not fired on us, we would not have killed him and his soldiers.

"Custer first shot and killed an Indian boy who was camped with his father a few miles below our village. The boy was helping his father skin a buffalo when the soldiers fired into their camp. The soldiers rode on, but the father jumped on his horse and hurried to tell us what had happened.[2]

"None of the Indians expected a fight. The children were swimming in the river and playing on the bank. The women were cooking and packing their stores as we planned to break camp.

"Far in the distance we saw a thick cloud of smoke. There was great fear and excitement among my people when we knew the soldiers were coming. We were not prepared to fight, and even when we saw the soldiers coming, we did not make ready for battle.

"Before Custer arrived, another band of soldiers attacked the lower end of the village, about three miles from Eagle Bear's tepee, he said. It was Reno's troops. The Indians there quickly drove them to refuge in a fringe of timber, where the soldiers stayed until Benteen's men came several hours later.

"When Custer's men drew near our camp they fired at us," Eagle Bear continued. "Many of our warriors rode into a ravine where Custer could not see them but through which he would have to pass to reach our village.

"Custer's men kept coming. My father sent me running to find my mother and sister who were digging wild turnips

---

[2]This is a reference to Deeds, although the narrator confuses this incident with another, the skinning of a buffalo on Reno Creek, possibly by Fast Horn, which incident had nothing to do with the killing of Deeds.

near the river. He told me to see that they fled to safety. They had already gone when I got there, so I hurried back. The fight with Custer was just starting.

"Our men, catching Custer by surprise, had driven him out of the ravine to the top of a small hill. I hurried to join the fighters. We could not ride in a circle around Custer's soldiers because they were on one edge of the hill. There were great numbers of us, some on horseback, others on foot. Back and forth in front of Custer we passed, firing all of the time. We were yelling and screaming. The soldiers were falling fast. Then we rode suddenly right into Custer's men and killed all who were still alive. The massacre did not last longer than fifteen minutes," Eagle Bear said.

"When the soldiers were dead, the young boys between the ages of 11 and 15 years old ran from one body to another, shooting arrows and firing rifles into them, scalping them and stripping their clothes. The boys were more cruel than the warriors.

"Only Custer's body went untouched. He was the chief and our people had great respect for the white man's chief."

Eagle Bear could not recall how many warriors were in the battle, but he believed there were several thousand. . . .

"Would you like to be a warrior again, live in big camps with your people, [and] fish and hunt?" It seemed a natural question to ask of the old Indian. Eagle Bear answered without hesitation. "When I was young, I liked to fight. But now that I'm old and it doesn't interest me any more, I am contented to live quietly here with my horses. . . ."

Epilogue

The George W. Glenn
Narrative Account

Editorial note: The George W. Glenn narrative is housed in the Walter Camp Collection, Little Bighorn Battlefield National Monument, Crow Agency, Montana, and it is reproduced hereafter with their permission.

George W. Glenn (1845–1914), alias George W. Glease, served in the Seventh Cavalry from 1875 till 1877. At the time of the Custer Battle he was a private in H Company and participated in the Reno Hill fight. In 1913 Glenn was asked by Walter M. Camp to write an account of his battle experiences. The resulting narrative which follows hereafter has been divided into paragraphs; spelling and grammatical errors have been corrected, and punctuation has been added when necessary. For additional information by Glenn, see his interview with Camp in Hammer, *Custer in '76*, pp. 135–37.

[THE] 1876 CAMPAIGN COMMANDED BY
GENERAL ALFRED TERRY

H and M Troop of the 7th US Cavalry received orders to leave Fort Rice [on May 5] and report at headquarters of the

7th Cavalry, Fort Lincoln, Dakota, where we went into camp with the regiment [on May 6]. We [had] not been in camp but a few days when the hostile scouts would come near camp [and] signified that they had declared war. Therefore the 7th Cavalry was ordered to take action against them. The regiment did not intend to leave Fort Lincoln so soon. The regiment broke camp the 17th day of May, having about twenty-five or thirty wagons with them. The steamer Far West was chartered to carry provisions and ordnance stores and to bring the wounded back if a battle should be fought.

The regiment passed through Bismarck, Dakota, at 10 A.M., accompanied by Mrs. George A. Custer and the US Paymaster. On arriving at Heart River, the Paymaster paid the regiment. This was done for fear that most of the regiment might be left back [drunk] in Bismarck. The regiment went to work building [a] pontoon bridge to cross the wagon train over the Heart River. It came upon a hard rain storm which made our movement slow in crossing the gumbo hills of Dakota, and the regiment did not reach the Little Missouri River until the last of May owing to a snow storm [blowing] through the night. The regiment was camped there until the fourth of June [June 3], then broke camp, making a dry camp between the Little Missouri and Powder River.

"Boots and Saddles" were sounded early on the morning of the 5th of June and [we] arrived at Powder River the evening of the 7th. There General Terry discovered an Indian trail. Terry sent his scouts to follow the trail, and from the direction it took, the scouts soon returned, stating that the Indians were moving in the direction of the Little Big Horn. Terry left his wagon train at Powder River [on June 15] and took his pack train with him, and all men [who] were not able to stand the trip were also left with the wagon train, besides a guard with the train. The number of men, including trumpeters, would amount to about one hundred men.

The column moved slowly up the Yellowstone River and on reaching Tongue River [on June 16] we found some Indian graves buried on [platforms on] stakes and in crotches of trees. The 7th Cavalry tore down these graves and threw them in Tongue River.[1] [This was] a most unwise act to disturb these dead, for I drank water about a hundred yards below where they were. One Indian that was lodged in the crotch of a tree had not been cut down and [did not] fall in the river. We [did] not go in camp there, so the column moved slowly up the Yellowstone River, having flankers out so the Indians could not lie in ambush for us. I wish to say there was a putrefied papoose at the foot of one of these trees who had fallen from one of the graves.

After a few days we reached the Rosebud Creek [on June 21]. There we found the steamer Far West tied up and also Colonel Gibbon with four troops of the 2nd Cavalry and the 7th Infantry. It was at the Rosebud where Custer received his orders. Custer was ordered to issue twelve pounds of oats and two horse shoes, one forefoot and one hind foot shoe which every man would carry on his horse with him. . . . Custer were to send Terry word at the mouth of the Little Big Horn by a scout when he had located the Indian village.

Custer left the mouth of the Rosebud Creek on the 24th of June [June 22]. In marching along the Rosebud we passed through a good many broken-up camps where the Indians were concentrating [prior to going] over to the Little Big

---

[1]These Indian graves were desecrated by G Company at the direction of General Custer. One of these sepulchers was fastened to a scaffold supported by four uprights, painted alternately black and red, indicating that the deceased had been a brave man. This scaffold was looted and dismantled, the body unwrapped, and then thrown into the river by Isaiah Dorman who was later seen fishing at the spot. General Custer himself, his brothers Tom and Boston, and his nephew, Harry A. Reed, all partook in the desecration in search of souvenirs such as weapons, bridles, beaded moccasins, and utensils. Harry A. Reed took a bow and six arrows, and a pair of moccasins from a sepulcher. It was said at the time among the Seventh's soldiers that the Custers and McIntosh's troop would be sorry for the looting, which prophecy was borne out by subsequent events.

Horn. We marched day and night. At midnight we would rest, holding our horses by the bridle, then continued our march until the morning of the 25th. Then [they] issued more ammunition. That was when Mitch Bouyer, the half-breed scout, returned [and] told Custer that the village contained from eight to ten thousand. Custer did not take any notice of what the scout had told him. Everyone knew what Custer would do: that Custer would go in and [that] Mitch Bouyer was willing to guide him; but Mitch Bouyer knew what would be the consequences. But Custer was a man that you could not dictate to. No one would know his plans.

Custer continued his march [to] within five miles of the Little Big Horn on the 25th of June and then made a halt. Custer gave Major Reno his orders. Custer told Reno that he, Custer, would pick up his five troops and go ahead, and Reno to keep up close in [the] rear with the remainder of the troops, and keep the pack train up also at the same time.[2] Custer had Mrs. Custer's horse Sadie on the trip with him in order to have a fresh horse [when] going into the battle.[3] Custer started on at a dash.

Reno [*sic*—Benteen] got off Custer's trail and went astray in the hills. On his return out of the hills he was met by Trum-

---

[2]Glenn's recollection probably refers to the division of Custer's regiment near the top of the divide, at noon, June 25, when the troops were divided into four battalions, commanded as follows: Capt. Benteen (Companies D, H, and K), Major Reno (Companies A, G, and M), Capt. Keogh (Companies C, I, and L), and Capt. Yates (Companies E and F). Capt. McDougall and Company B escorted the pack train in the rear of the regiment.

[3]Glenn's statement that Custer had brought his wife's horse Sadie on the campaign receives corroboration from Emma Reed who wrote that Elizabeth's pony was taken along on the expedition. However, the thought of the General riding a pony at the head of his regiment seems ludicrous to me, especially since he had at his disposal Vic and Dandy. I assume, therefore, that this pony was brought along for the benefit of one of Custer's family members. Since Harry A. Reed rode a pony named Dick, according to Tom Custer, I speculate that Boston Custer may have ridden Elizabeth's pony Sadie. In fact, Boston Custer had two ponies, one of which he had lent to Pvt. William Hardden of D Company.

peter [John] Martin[4] with a dispatch to ["]Come quick and bring packs; big village,["] but for some unaccountable reason Reno did not follow Custer's trail, but Reno switched off Custer's trail four miles up the Little Horn, and on the left of the village. After arriving on the bluffs facing the river, he undertook to go down the river to join Custer, but seeing so many Indians between him and Custer, he saw that he was completely cut off. Benteen advised Reno to fall back and corral his pack train in the ravine.

By this time Custer was in the fight. Custer had his charge about 2:30 [P.M.]. Reno had his charge about 3 o'clock. After Reno had crossed the river, he saw so many Indians coming out of the timber [that] he dismounted his men to fight on foot formations. The last time he mounted his men they all struck a panic and retreated back to the ford of the river where they had crossed. At the same time the Indians were shooting his men out of their saddles. Reno lost heavy on this charge in the valley.

After the retreat back to the hills, H Troop held one bluff and the other troops held the back of [the] other hills. It was not long after Reno was surrounded before the Indians led a charge on H Troop. Their point was to get the hill that H Troop held. If they had got that hill they would [have] massacred every man of Reno's command. They did three or four charges and none got the hill. The last charge was [such] a hard one that Benteen was compelled to call on Reno for reinforcement. M Troop was sent to Benteen's rescue and repulsed the Indians.

When we would have time we dug holes in the ground so we could get our heads out of sight. It seems we did not care

---

[4]Trumpeter John Martin, born Giovanni Martini (1851–1922), enlisted in H Company in 1874 and retired in 1904 with the rank of sergeant, having served the majority of his military years with the artillery branch of the Army. During the Sioux campaign of 1876, Martin was assigned to headquarters' staff as trumpeter orderly to Custer.

for any other part of the body. We used our butcher knives as we could not find any picks nor shovels at the time of the fight. I think we did well to hold them off with what few men [we had] against such [a] large force of Indians, for when Custer's command was massacred, every Indian came on Reno.

H Troop ran out ammunition on the hill. Every man looked upon another to see who would go in the ravine where the pack train was to get ammunition. I saw that nobody would go, so myself and a comrade [named] Jones went down after a box. After that comrade [Julien D.] Jones[5] was killed. I could not carry a box of carbine ammunition, so I carried a box of pistol cartridges, and on my way up the hill from the ravine a bullet struck the box that I carried. There must have been [a total of] three or four bullets [that] struck it. I fell to the ground, pretending that I was dead, playing possum on the Indians. Benteen told some of the men to run down the hill and get the box I carried. I spoke in a low voice that I was only resting [and that] I would be there in a minute [or] so.

When I arrived on top of the hill the Indians led another charge. That [was] the charge that nearly drove H Troop from the hill. This charge was on the evening of the 25th. The charge on the morning of the 26th was not a bad one. I pitied the poor wounded who were lying among the pack train that were shot down for the protection of the wounded, for they were suffering for water. We broke open boxes of tomatoes and other fruits, which were officers' fruits, and gave them to the wounded to stop their thirst until such time we could get water for them. There was a water party selected to get water

---

[5]Pvt. Julien D. Jones (1849–1876) enlisted in H Company in 1871. He participated in the Reno Hill Fight and was one of ten men who defended the "horseshoe (southern) position" on Reno Hill on June 26. He volunteered to bring ammunition to H Company's line and completed this dangerous task safely, but was subsequently killed in his trench while taking off his coat by a bullet which passed through several hardtack boxes.

for them, protected by a firing party along the ridge, with orders from Captain Benteen to give no man water but only the wounded, [and to] let every man get his own water.

We held the Indians off all day on the 26th. At night things were quieter. It was on the evening of the 25th [afternoon on the 26th] when Madden of D [K] Troop lost his leg.[6] It was cut off on top of the hill. There were not many shots fired from the Indians on the morning of the 27th. It looked to me [that] if Terry were a dashing man like Custer, he could [have] come up on the 26th instead of the 27th, for Terry had only twenty miles to come. However, when Terry came up to Reno he asked Reno where General Custer was. Reno replied that he did not know. Last [thing] he heard from Custer's men . . . [was] firing down the river at sundown on the evening of the 25th. It seems that Terry came through Custer's battlefield for Terry told Reno to take all his picks and shovels and bury the dead [of] Custer's massacred command.

Terry took care of Reno's wounded while Reno was tracing up Custer's dead. It looked to me that it was a running fight as the dead looked that way from the way the men lay when they were found. There is no picture of the fight . . . [that shows] the bodies the way they lay on the ridge for we had not any photographer with us, and the reporter was killed. Only a sketch can be given of the fight of Custer's men

---

[6]Born in 1836, Saddler Michael P. Madden enlisted in the Seventh Cavalry in 1866 and served in K Company at the time of the 1876 campaign. While attempting to get water for the wounded on June 26, Madden sustained a gunshot would to the right leg which fractured the bones just below the knee, necessitating amputation the next day. Lt. Godfrey later recalled that Madden was one of the coolest soldiers and one of the best marksmen in the regiment. Although Godfrey recommended him for a Medal of Honor, the Officers Merit Board did not endorse the recommendation and a medal was thus not awarded. However, Madden was promoted to sergeant on July 12, 1876, with a retroactive date to June 26. According to Sgt. John Ryan and Pvt. William Slaper, Madden was later promoted to Regimental Saddler and served at the Harness Depot at the departmental headquarters at St. Paul. Although he was described by Sgt. Ryan as a good-natured individual, Lt. Luther R. Hare remembered Madden as an alcoholic for whom no one had much respect.

by the men that helped to bury the dead. I will give the historian the whole thing of Custer's dead.

It seems that Custer's men never crossed the river. We found [a] trail going down in the river, but it seems that Custer got repulsed before he got across the river . . . [because] we never found any trail of him on the other side of the river. The first men were found on the ridge, and on a little knoll was the Chief Trumpeter with three arrows in his head and one in his right shoulder.[7] The next was [Mark] Kellogg, the New York reporter, [who lay] about 50 yards from the Chief Trumpeter [and] who only had arrows in his body.[8] [Then came] first a [single] horse and then there were ten or twelve horses and their riders. Most all of these men were mutilated and nearly all had arrows put in them.

Further up the ridge we found scattering soldiers and their horses. Thomas Tweed of L Troop was a young man that I enlisted with. He was cut up the crotch and his left leg thrown over his left shoulder and he had three arrows in his face, but

---

[7]Testimony is at variance as to the kill site of Chief Trumpeter Henry Voss. According to Pvt. August DeVoto, Voss was found a mile from Custer's battlefield, propped in a kneeling position, with his rear riddled with arrows. According to Blacksmith Henry W. B. Mechling, the body lay near the river, about 200 yards from the cut bank near Deep Ravine. This statement agrees with Pvt. Glenn who later recalled that the remains were found near the ford, within a stone's throw of the river. However, Pvt. Dennis Lynch was certain that Voss was found near Custer on the hilltop, which statement is corroborated by Pvt. August B. Seifert. Further confirmation is provided by Thomas F. O'Neill who stated that Voss was found on the hill, the body laying facedown across the head of Sgt. John H. Vickory, who lay faceup. The kill site location of Voss is further corroborated by Trumpeter David McVeigh who stated that Voss' body was found within twelve feet of the remains of Lt. William W. Cooke.

In retrospect, it is possible that the body found near the river and allegedly identified by Glenn, DeVoto, and Mechling as Chief Trumpeter Henry Voss, may have been, and probably was, the body of Trumpeter Henry C. Dose. According to several witnesses, Trumpeter Dose was found near the river, on the south bank of Deep Ravine, his body riddled with arrows in the sides and back.

[8]Mark Kellogg (1833–1876) was a reporter for the *Bismarck Tribune*. His remains were discovered by Col. John Gibbon who found the body lying on its back near the river, fully dressed, in an advanced state of decomposition. He was scalped and one ear had been cut off. Identification was confirmed through the peculiar shape of one of his boots. Kellogg's remains were interred by Lt. Edward G. Mathey on June 29.

was not scalped.[9] They had not time to scalp all of these men for there [were] about 280 [*sic*] men that were killed on the ridge. There was not any horse with Tweed, but there was a horse that had been wounded and [still] alive not far from Tweed.

Further up the ridge and at the head of the ridge, Captain Benteen rode ahead and [after] looking in the ravine, turned around and said to Major Reno, "Here is the whole Headquarters." [We found] part of C Troop and part of E Troop, besides General Custer, Captain T. Custer, Captain Keogh, Captain Calhoun, the brother-in-law of Custer, [and] Captain Yates. I am not certain of Yates. Lieutenant Sturgis' trousers were found but we did not find the body at that time. Custer's nephew [was killed and was] about 18 years old. The list of troops with Custer are C, E, F, I [and] L. . . . Captain Keogh [and] Sturgis belonged to M Troop but were with E Troop when they were killed. Lieutenant DeRudio, an Italian officer [who] was Italian but held a commission in the 7th Cavalry, escaped from Custer's [command]. No doubt he got across the river because he came from the timber up to Reno's command on the 26th.

After we buried Custer's men we crossed the river where the Indian village had stood. We found two heads of men that were captured from Major Reno's command when Reno led his charge the evening of the 25th. I think they were captured on the 25th because we heard the powwow in the village. One of the heads was recognized to be [that] of [John E.] Armstrong, A Troop, 7th Cavalry. The head was identified by Captain Moylan of A Troop. This Armstrong belonged to Moylan's troop that was under Reno's command.[10]

---

[9]Pvt. Thomas S. Tweed (1853–1876) of L Company. He enlisted in 1875 and was nicknamed "Boss."

[10]Pvt. John E. Armstrong (1836–1876) enlisted in A Company in 1875 and was killed during the retreat from the valley. After the battle his decapitated body was found in the bottoms near the remains of Isaiah Dorman. His scorched head, however, was discovered in one of the lower camps, stuck on top of a pole. The head was identified by Capt. Myles Moylan who commanded Armstrong's company.

We buried the two heads [and] then moved up the river to General Terry's camp to prepare a way to carry our wounded to the mouth of the Little Big Horn and place them on board the steamer Far West. We took the Indian lodge poles that they left [and], besides, we cut some poles from the timber and made stretchers. They issued out rations in order to get Col. Gibbon's pack mules [unloaded]. We put a mule in front and rear [of the stretcher] and then attached the poles to the mules. Then we put the wounded on the stretchers. The 7th Infantry would march on each [side] of the stretchers to keep it steady. We nearly took all night marching to the mouth of the Little Big Horn. Some died on the way after the wounded were on board the steamer.

The command pulled out for the mouth of the Bighorn River where we waited for a few days to hear from General Crook. Word reached camp that Crook [was] over on the Rosebud Creek. Terry packed up at once and moved over to where Crook was in camp and held council with him to [decide] what to do. They came to the conclusion not to follow the Indian trail, but to go over to the Powder River where the 7th Cavalry [had] left their wagon train. On arriving at Powder River we found that the wagons had been destroyed and the grain was scattered all over the ground and the escorts all killed.[11]

[After] we buried the dead, General Terry and Crook separated. Terry went to Fort Lincoln to recruit the 7th Cavalry to replace the five troops that were lost the 25th of June, 1876. Crook went down to the lower agencies to disarm the Indians. After the 7th Cavalry was filled up they went down the

---

[11]On August 2, 1876, two companies of the Sixth Infantry and one company of the Seventh Infantry, commanded by Major Orlando H. Moore, were attacked by Indians while salvaging seventy-five tons of grain cached at the abandoned Powder River Depot. The Indians were driven off with the aid of a Napoleon Gun and sustained only one casualty during the fight. Contrary to Glenn's belief, no wagons were destroyed and only one civilian was killed, a scout by the name of Brockmeyer.

river to the Standing Rock agency to disarm the Indians on that reservation. We went through their lodges, cutting up their lariats [and] breaking up their saddles, and after this was done we drove their ponies off. Then we returned to our headquarters [at] Fort Lincoln, Dakota.[12]

General Custer has been severely criticized for the failure of this campaign, and it seems justly so as he disobeyed [orders] in not sending word to General Terry when he located their village, and [for] bringing on the battle on the 25th instead of the 26th, and [for] not taking the Gatling guns and the four troops of the 2nd Cavalry, as he was ordered. The plan of this campaign was for Custer to move up the Rosebud and [for] Terry to move up the Little Horn River, and Crook was to come in the rear of the Indians, and all be connected together. If this was done the day would [have] been ours.[13]

This article was written by a survivor of Major Reno's command that was in the disastrous campaign, George W. Glease, H Troop, 7th US Cavalry, at the Battle of the Little Big Horn, June the 25th, 1876. My actual name is George W. Glenn, Company B, National Soldiers Home, Hampton, Virginia.

---

[12]Pursuant to orders from the War Department in October 1876, units from the Seventh Cavalry and Seventeenth Infantry marched to the agencies at Standing Rock and Cheyenne River to disarm hostile Sioux bands. In addition to a variety of arms, some 2,100 ponies were confiscated and taken to St. Paul, to be sold at an auction to benefit the Indians. Only 700 ponies would eventually reach St. Paul, the rest having "disappeared" along the shipping route. This seizure resulted in a public outcry which eventually compelled the Congress to appropriate funds to repay the Sioux Indians.

[13]For General Terry's orders, and Walter M. Camp's scholarly comments thereon, see the appendix hereafter.

The August L. DeVoto Narrative

Editorial note: The August L. DeVoto narrative was appended to a letter written by DeVoto to Walter M. Camp, dated October 1, 1917, which is contained in the Walter Camp Collection, Little Bighorn Battlefield National Monument, Crow Agency, Montana. It is reproduced hereafter with their permission.

August L. DeVoto (1852–1923) served with the Seventh Cavalry from 1873 till 1878. At the time of the Custer Battle, DeVoto was a private in B Company and participated in the Reno Hill Fight. The transcript which follows was made from the typewritten original.

Description of Reno's Fight

On the 22nd of June, 1876, the 7th United States Cavalry was camped on the Yellowstone River, near the mouth of the Rosebud Creek.

That afternoon General Custer, in command, left General Terry and started up the Rosebud, to go and make short work of Sitting Bull and his band of Indians. We had no wagons to haul supplies, so [we] used pack mules; we had about one hundred and fifty mules. We soldiers did the packing and took care of the mules.

We traveled up the Rosebud all that day until nearly dark. The next day, the 23rd, we started out at about five o'clock in the morning, and travelled all that day until dark. The morning of the 24th, we started upstream and struck the Indian trail, which was getting larger and larger as we went along. That afternoon we got near the head of the Rosebud. We camped there that night. We broke camp that night between twelve and one o'clock; it was so dark that I could scarcely see the man riding in front of me. His mule had some camp kettles strapped on the pack saddle, and I followed the noise made by the kettles hitting against the saddle. We travelled that way until about daylight and then halted for a rest. We slept about an hour.

The morning of the 25th we started out again. My troop, Troop B, was in the advance, Captain T. M. McDougall in command. After we had arrived within about ten miles of the Indian camp, we halted for about a half hour rest. Here the Officer's Call was sounded. This must have been the time General Custer made his final plan of attack on the Indians, taking five troops with him under his immediate command, assigning three troops to Major Reno, three troops to Captain Benteen, and one troop [as] rear guard (Troop B). Before the command moved, the men from each troop were detailed to take charge of the pack train of mules. I was one of the ten from my troop. Inasmuch as my troop had been advance guard our mules were placed ahead of the pack train.

General Custer and his five troops went on ahead, also Major Reno and Captain Benteen. It seems the plan was to get the Indians between two fires, for Reno crossed the river above the Indian camp and made the first attack with the three troops under his command. Custer with his five troops went farther west. The Indians, of which there was a very large number, must have dismounted and concealed themselves in the dry ravine, for when we buried Custer and his men I noticed there were no dead Indian ponies.

Getting back now to the starting place with the pack mules, as I stated before, we were ahead of the train, and kept moving pretty lively. We passed a tepee in which there was a dead Indian. Presently we began to hear firing. Soon afterward we met a Crow Indian coming from the direction General Custer had gone. He could not talk much English. We asked him how about the soldiers. He made motions with his hands, saying, "Much soldiers down," no doubt meaning soldiers killed.

We next met a soldier from Custer's command. Custer had sent him with a message to Major Reno.[1] It seems the fight had not yet started when Custer sent him, as he said nothing about it.

Presently we were in plain view of the Indian camp. We were on a hill and the Indian camp looked beautiful in the green valley. After travelling a little closer we could see Major Reno and his command slowly climbing up the hill. I went over to a man of G Troop by the name of [Hugh] McGonigal[2] [sic] and asked him what had happened. He said Major Reno had retreated from the Indians and had lost a considerable number of men. He said Lieutenant McIntosh had been killed and that Lieutenant Hodgson was missing. The doctor had been killed just as he reached the top of the hill.[3] He was the first of the command that I had seen dead.

---

[1]Since there were two messengers dispatched from Custer's command, we cannot be certain of the identity of the one spoken of by DeVoto. It may have been Sgt. Daniel A. Kanipe of C Company who was sent by Capt. Thomas Custer with verbal instructions for Capt. Thomas McDougall to hurry the pack train to the front. Or, it could have been Trumpeter John Martin who was dispatched shortly after Kanipe with a written message for Capt. Frederick Benteen to hurry to the front and to bring along the packs.

[2]Pvt. Hugh McGonigle (1838–1914) enlisted in G Company in 1872 and was one of thirteen troopers left behind in the timber during the retreat from the valley. McGonigle was said to have been a stepson of Major Marcus A. Reno.

[3]Dr. James M. DeWolf (1843–1876) was killed near the top of the bluff on the east side of the river during the retreat from the valley. Examination of his body revealed a gunshot wound to the chest and four bullet wounds in his face, the latter inflicted by his own revolver. He was buried by Dr. Henry R. Porter on June 26.

In the meantime Captain Benteen came along with his three troops, also the pack train, and finally B Troop, the rear guard. Shortly after the rear guard came up a lieutenant from A Troop [Charles A. Varnum], Sergeant [Benjamin C.] Criswell,[4] two other men and myself were detailed to go find Lieutenant Hodgson. We had gone about half way down the hill towards the river when an orderly came and told us to come back. When we got back D Troop started out in the direction General Custer was supposed to be. The whole command had been strung out when D Troop came back at a charge gait. The officers must have noticed that we were being surrounded. We moved east about half a mile and the command was dismounted. The ground was well chosen. We were close to the edge of the hill and had a good look-out toward the river on the south and east, and north and west was open country. That gave the Indians no place for concealment; besides there was a sort of depression in the ground which gave protection to the horses and mules. Almost before the troops were formed the fight commenced. It kept up until dark. Shortly after the firing ceased someone sounded taps, but not from our camp. This must have been a ruse of the Indians to make us believe that Custer was camped nearby. When we buried Custer's men we found his chief bugler's body about a mile away from Custer's battlefield, all alone and stark naked. His body was in a kneeling position and his back was stuck full of arrows.[5]

On the morning of the 26th, the fight commenced at daybreak and was swift and furious. We fought until about noon. I believe the Indians were getting short of ammunition about

[4]Sgt. Benjamin C. Criswell (1849–1921) enlisted in B Company in 1870 and was promoted from corporal to sergeant on June 4, 1876. He was a brother of Pvt. Harry Criswell who was also of B Company.

[5]The Chief Trumpeter was Henry Voss. However, DeVoto may have been mistaken about his identification and might have confused Voss with Trumpeter Henry C. Dose who was also assigned to Headquarters' Staff. See footnote 7, Glenn Narrative Account.

this time. Our wounded men began calling for water and about a dozen of us volunteered to go to the river and get it. We went down to the river, the ravine protecting us from being exposed to the Indians. When we got to the bottom of the ravine there was an open space of about twenty feet to the bank of the creek. This was very dangerous as it gave Mr. Indian an excellent chance to shoot from his place of concealment on the opposite side of the creek. We each carried as many canteens as we possibly could. It takes quite a little time to fill a canteen, besides we knew it would mean sure death to stand by the bank to fill them. However, one of the boys had carried down a big camp kettle. The thought struck me that it would be much safer to wade in the stream and get the kettle full of water, and then run back under cover to fill the canteens. I did this. One man by the name of [Michael P.] Madden attempted to fill his canteen at the creek and was shot in the leg. His leg was amputated the next day by Dr. Plumer [Henry R. Porter]. I think that was the Doctor's name. The only other doctor we had had been killed, as before stated.

Along about four o'clock in the afternoon the Indians moved away. We did not follow them. That evening we watered the horses and mules for the first time since the fight, took up more ground, and had bacon, coffee and hardtack, the first since the morning of the 25th.

The next day, the 27th, some of us were detailed to go over Reno's battleground and find the missing or dead. I with Sergeant Criswell and three other men went to look for Lieutenant [Benjamin H.] Hodgson.[6] We found his body on the bank about twenty feet from the water. His body was

---

[6]This squad of soldiers was commanded by Sgt. Benjamin C. Criswell and consisted of Saddler John A. Bailey and Privates Thomas W. Coleman, Augustus L. DeVoto, and Stephen L. Ryan. Of these five men, only two were recommended by McDougall for the Medal of Honor, namely Criswell and Ryan. However, only Criswell was awarded the coveted medal for recovering Hodgson's body within the enemy lines, for bringing ammo to the trenches, and for encouraging the men in the most exposed positions on the firing line.

naked. He had been shot in the temple and groin. Nearby were several dead members of G Troop. One, I remember, was Sergeant [Edward] Botzer, First Sergeant of G Troop.[7] We laid Lieutenant Hodgson's body across our carbines and carried it to camp. We dug a grave, wrapped his body in a blanket, and buried it on the hill. We planted a sapling there to mark his grave.

All this time we did not know what had become of Custer and his men, never thinking that he and all of them had been slaughtered. Along about noon we saw a cloud of dust in the west and thought the Indians were coming back. We were prepared to receive them, but discovered that it was General Terry and his command. They brought us the sad news that Custer and his men had all been killed. The next day we went over the battlefield and buried them. It was sickening and sad.

Afterwards we went over the ground where the Indian camp had been. There were two tepees left standing full of dead Indians. As we rode past I looked in. They were piled up like cordwood.[8] One of them looked to me very much like a white man. I could not see his face, but his legs looked white. I had no chance to go in and make a close investigation.

We then skinned a lot of dead horses and mules and cut the hide in narrow strips, chopped down a lot of young saplings, and made litters. In the evening we put a mule in front and one behind, and put litters on the animals' backs,

---

[7]Sgt. Edward Botzer enlisted in G Company in 1866 and served as trumpeter until 1871. After his reenlistment, he advanced to the rank of sergeant and was appointed Acting First Sergeant upon the furlough of First Sgt. Edward Garlick on April 14, 1876.

[8]Of those officers who investigated the contents of these lodges, Capt. Walter Clifford and Lt. Charles F. Roe later stated they counted only eight bodies, Lt. Winfield S. Edgerly recalled eleven, Dr. Holmes O. Paulding counted sixteen, while Lt. Richard E. Thompson remembered seeing twenty-two.

two men leading them. In this manner we took the wounded, about fifty, to the mouth of the Little Big Horn River where the steamer Far West was waiting to take the wounded to Fort Abraham Lincoln. We travelled all night on the banks of the Big Horn. After sending the wounded away we travelled down the Big Horn River to the mouth of the Yellowstone. We crossed the river here in a boat and camped at what was called Fort Pease.[9] Here we got new supplies. We then travelled on down until we got opposite the Rosebud. Here we again crossed the Yellowstone River and drew clothing and rations and started out again. On our second day out we met General [George] Crook's command.[10] Buffalo Bill, his Chief Scout, was with him.

The 7th Cavalry and Crook's command moved together for about three days, when they discovered that the Indians had disbanded and some had gone into Canada. The two commands then separated, the 7th Cavalry going to the mouth of the Tongue River on the Yellowstone. We camped here about three weeks.

.   .   .   .

This ends the expedition of the Little Big Horn, except about one week after we made a short trip down the river to Standing Rock, and took a lot of ponies away from the Indians, and drove them to Fort Lincoln.

---

[9]Fort Pease was built in 1875 by F. D. Pease and a party of traders from Bozeman, Montana. Being continuously harassed by the Sioux and failing in its economic objective, the fort was abandoned by its remaining occupants in March of the following year.

[10]This union with Crook's troops took place on August 10, 1876, along the Rosebud, some thirty miles down from its mouth.

Appendix A
General Terry's Letter of Instructions[1]

Headquarters Department of Dakota
(In the Field)
Camp at Mouth of Rosebud River
Montana Territory, June 22nd 1876.
Lieut. Col. G. A. Custer, 7th Cavalry.

Colonel:

The Brigadier-General Commanding directs that, as soon as your regiment can be made ready for the march, you will proceed up the Rosebud in pursuit of the Indians whose trail was discovered by Major Reno a few days since. It is, of course, impossible to give you any definite instructions in regard to this movement, and were it not impossible to do so, the Department Commander places too much confidence in your zeal, energy, and ability to wish to impose upon you precise orders which might hamper your action when nearly in contact with the enemy. He will, however, indicate to you his own views of what your action should be, and he desires that you should conform to them unless you shall see sufficient

---

[1]Copy in author's collection

reason for departing from them. He thinks that you should proceed up the Rosebud until you ascertain definitely the direction in which the trail above spoken of leads. Should it be found (as it appears almost certain that it will be found) to turn towards the Little Horn, he thinks that you should still proceed southward, perhaps as far as the headwaters of the Tongue, and then turn towards the Little Horn, feeling constantly, however, to your left, so as to preclude the possibility of the escape of the Indians to the south or southeast by passing around your left flank.

The column of Colonel Gibbon is now in motion for the mouth of the Big Horn. As soon as it reaches that point it will cross the Yellowstone and move up at least as far as the forks of the Big and Little Horns. Of course its further movements must be controlled by circumstances as they arise, but it is hoped that the Indians, if upon the Little Horn, may be so nearly inclosed by the two columns that their escape will be impossible. The Department Commander desires that on the way up the Rosebud you shall thoroughly examine the upper part of Tullock's Creek, and that you should endeavor to send a scout through to Colonel Gibbon's column, with information of the results of your examination. The lower part of the creek will be examined by a detachment from Colonel Gibbon's command.

The supply steamer will be pushed up the Big Horn as far as the forks if the river is found to be navigable for that distance, and the Department Commander, who will accompany the Column of Colonel Gibbon, desires you to report to him there not later than the expiration of the time for which your troops are rationed, unless in the meantime you receive further orders.

Very Respectfully,
Your obedient Servant,
Ed. W. Smith, Captain, 18th Infantry,
Acting Assistant Adjutant General.

Appendix B
Walter M. Camp's Comments on Terry's Instructions[1]

7740 Union Ave.,
Chicago, Ill.,
Sept. 18, 1918.

Gen. E.S. Godfrey,
Cookstown, N.J.

My Dear General:—

In your letter of 15th inst. you ask if I ever knew of Gen. Freeman making a statement to the effect that he heard or overheard Gen. Terry tell Gen. Custer that the latter might attack when he should meet the Indians.

No, I never heard that Gen. Freeman claimed to have heard such or to have been impressed that Terry told Custer at the parting that he might attack. I had considerable corre-

---

[1] Copy in author's collection. Walter Mason Camp (1867–1925) was an avid student of the Plains Indian Wars and was known among his contemporaries as the foremost authority on the battle of the Little Bighorn. In a span of about twenty years, Camp interviewed close to 200 individuals who in some way were connected with the Little Bighorn affair, among whom were officers and soldiers, scouts and interpreters, steamboat personnel, telegraph operators, enlisted Indian Scouts, and Sioux and Cheyenne warriors.

spondence with Gen. Freeman concerning the campaign of 1876 and talked with him personally once on the same subject, but he never mentioned that phase of the matter to me.

One of Gen. Freeman's associate officers of that year, Gen. Roe, might know something about this. I have had many personal interviews with Gen. Roe and have found him very well informed on what transpired at the time of the meeting at the mouth of the Rosebud just previous to your departure from there on June 22.

This raises a question that I have thought about and studied over a good deal, and I am going to give you some of my conclusions. Should you deem it the right thing to criticize them, frankly I will be delighted.

I refer to the old question as to whether or not Gen. Custer attacked the Indians on the Little Bighorn in disobedience of Gen. Terry's order. The order was a written one, and, according to my understanding of English, it was left to Custer's discretion as to whether or not he should attack should he encounter the Indians. He did encounter them, and I think he did the logical thing, as well as obeying Terry's order, in attacking them without waiting for Terry and Gibbon to come up. Whether Custer's plan, in detail, for attacking the village was the proper one is another question, but Terry's order had nothing to do with that.

The proposition that it were possible for Custer to have struck one side of the village, at the same time waiting for Terry and Gibbon to have come upstream and attacked them on the other side, I do not consider worthy of even academic standing. The Indians were well aware of the presence of Gibbon's troops on the Yellowstone all that spring and summer—in fact they had attacked him or some of his detachments several times in April or May, had killed stragglers from his command, and one night in April or May had crossed to the north side of the Yellowstone and run off a considerable herd of horses that were part of Gibbon's column. In fact the Indians were watching Gibbon all the time, knew where he was all the time, and it would have been impossible for him to have slipped up on them unaware from the direction of the Yellowstone by way of the Bighorn. They were also watching Crook from the other direction, but were not looking for any movement from the direction of the Rosebud, as some of them were camped on the Rosebud, themselves, within four or five days of the fight. When Terry and Gibbon did move up the Bighorn the Indian scouts encountered them some 30 miles down, as you know.

Now suppose that Custer had adopted the alternative suggested in Terry's order, and which Terry seemed to have thought the wiser course, namely, to have kept on to the head of the Rosebud, crossed over to the Little Bighorn and come down it. Such a detour would have involved two days of hard marching, or three days of ordinary marching, with cavalry and pack outfit, longer than actually was consumed in reaching the village, and the Indian scouts who were watching Crook (whom they fought only eight days previously) would surely have discovered Custer's assumed movement down the Little Bighorn, and the big camp would have fled across to the Rosebud and down it, just as it did five weeks later when Crook followed it toward the Yellowstone and across to the Little Missouri. In that event Custer would have been blamable for having left a hot trail leading to the Little Bighorn, direct from where Busby now is, in order to cut a big circuit around by the headwaters of the Rosebud and the Little Bighorn.

It is clear enough that the intent in Terry's order in the idea of suggesting this detour to Custer was that when Custer did encounter the Indians, he (Custer) should be on the side of them that was opposite from Terry, or, in other words, that the two commands should approach the Indians from opposite directions. This Custer really did accomplish, as the matter turned out, and so he fully carried out every specification in Terry's order.

But what happened? Did the Indians stampede from Custer down the stream? Not at all. They knew well enough that Gibbon's troops were in that direction. The women who left the village in large numbers when Reno attacked started west toward the Bighorn, to await developments, and when the whole village moved it went up the stream in the direction of Crook, whose exact location was known to them. They hung around the headwaters of the Tongue and Little Bighorn, within 20 miles of Crook, for a month or more, running buffalo, and occasionally burning up the grazing close to Crook's camp, finally going off down the Rosebud a few days in advance of Crook's march down that stream, as above stated.

Now, from the many interviews that I have had with these Indians, it is known that the gathering of the big village that Custer struck on the Little Bighorn was purely accidental. The Indians tell me that, from sheer necessity of subsistence for people and horses, the village would have had to break up or scatter out within the next two or three days. They knew of the presence of troops both to the north and to the south of them, were watching in both directions, and were not expecting a fight where it did come off. They were entirely off their guard toward the east, but neither Custer nor Terry could have gotten anywhere near their camp from the direction which Terry proposed in his order; that is, from down and up the Little Bighorn.

As to the best plan for catching up with the Indians, Custer's judgement was certainly correct. The trouble was that when he did catch them he did not have men enough to handle them. By taking another day and running the chance of being discovered he might have gained better knowledge of the strength of the village, in a night's scouting, but by that time the Indians would have been aware of Terry's approach, as was actually the case (on June 26), and then both Custer and Terry, with Gibbon, would have been in the stern chase. To think of cornering the Indians in such a big, open country was simply hopeless. Unless they would elect to stand and fight there would be no battle.

Yours sincerely,

[Signed:] W.M. Camp

Bibliography

Archival Sources

Berkeley, California. University of California Library. Bancroft Collection: The Oscar F. Long Papers.

Billings, Montana. Billings Public Library. Billings Clipping File.

Bloomington, Indiana. University of Indiana Library. Manuscripts Division. Robert S. Ellison Collection: Walter M. Camp Manuscripts.

Crow Agency, Montana. Little Bighorn Battlefield National Monument, National Park Service. Walter M. Camp Collection; Elizabeth B. Custer Collection.

Denver, Colorado. Colorado Historical Society. George Bent Manuscript Collection.

_____. Denver Public Library. Western History Division. Robert S. Ellison Collection: Walter Mason Camp Papers.

Laramie, Wyoming. University of Wyoming Library. Western History Research Center. Special Collections: Agnes W. Spring Collection.

Lincoln, Nebraska. Nebraska State Historical Society. Eli S. Ricker Collection.

Los Angeles, California. National History Museum. Western History Research Collections: Edward Curtis Papers.

————. Southwest Museum Library. Manuscripts Division: George B. Grinnell Collection.

Norman, Oklahoma. University of Oklahoma Library. Western History Collection: Walter S. Campbell Collection.

Provo, Utah. Brigham Young University Library. Manuscripts Division: Walter Mason Camp Manuscripts; Special Collections.

Topeka, Kansas. Kansas State Historical Society. Joseph G. Masters Collection.

Washington, D.C. National Archives. Record Group 94: Records of the Adjutant General's Department.

Printed Sources—Books

Berthrong, Donald J. *The Southern Cheyennes*. Norman: University of Oklahoma Press, 1963.

Blish, Helen H. *A Pictographic History of the Oglala Sioux*. Lincoln: University of Nebraska Press, 1967.

Bourke, John G. *On the Border with Crook*. New York: Charles Scribner's, 1891.

Boyes, William. *Custer's Black White Man*. Washington, D.C.: South Capitol Press, 1972.

————. *Surgeon's Diary*. Rockville: WJBM Associates, 1974.

Brown, Mark H. and W. R. Felton. *The Frontier Years: L. A. Huffman, Photographer of the Plains*. New York: Henry Holt, 1955.

Buecker, Thomas R. and R. Eli Paul. *The Crazy Horse Surrender Ledger*. Lincoln: University of Nebraska Press, 1994.

Burdick, Usher L. *Tales from the Buffalo Land*. Baltimore: Wirth Brothers, 1940.

_____. *David F. Barry's Indian Notes on the Custer Battle.*
Baltimore: Wirth Brothers, 1949.

Carroll, John M. *The Benteen-Goldin Letters on Custer and His Last Battle.* New York: Liveright, 1974.

Chandler, Melbourne C. *Of Garry Owen in Glory: The History of the Seventh United States Cavalry Regiment.* Annandale, CA: privately printed, 1960.

Crawford, Lewis F. *Rekindling Camp Fires: The Exploits of Ben Arnold.* Bismarck, ND: Capitol Book Co., 1926.

Curtis, Edward S. *The North American Indians, III.* Cambridge: The University Press, 1908.

Custer, George A. *My Life on the Plains.* Lincoln: University of Nebraska Press, 1966.

DeBarthe, Joe. *Life and Adventures of Frank Grouard.* Norman: University of Oklahoma Press, 1958.

DeMallie, Raymond J. *The Sixth Grandfather: Black Elk's Teachings Given to John G. Neihardt.* Lincoln: University of Nebraska Press, 1984.

Dixon, Joseph K. *The Vanishing Race.* New York: Bonanza Books, 1975.

Finerty, John F. *War-path and Bivouac: The Bighorn and Yellowstone Expedition.* Chicago: The Lakeside Press, 1955.

Fox, Richard Allan, Jr. *Archaeology, History, and Custer's Last Battle.* Norman: University of Oklahoma Press, 1993.

Graham, W. A. *The Custer Myth: A Source Book of Custeriana.* New York: Bonanza Books, 1953.

_____. *Abstract of the Official Record of the Reno Court of Inquiry.* Harrisburg: Stackpole, 1954

Gray, John S. *Centennial Campaign: The Sioux War of 1876.* Fort Collins, CO: Old Army Press, 1976.

Grinnell, George Bird. *The Fighting Cheyennes.* Norman: University of Oklahoma Press, 1956.

_____. *The Cheyenne Indians.* 2 vols. Lincoln: University of Nebraska Press, 1972.

Hammer, Kenneth. *Men with Custer*. Fort Collins, CO: Old Army Press, 1972.

_____. *Men with Custer: Biographies of the 7th Cavalry*. Hardin, MT: Custer Battlefield Historical and Museum Association, Inc., 1995.

_____. *Custer in '76: Walter Camp's Notes on the Custer Fight*. Provo, UT: Brigham Young University Press, 1976.

Hardorff, Richard G. *Markers, Artifacts, and Indian Testimony: Preliminary Findings on the Custer Battle*. Short Hills, NJ: Don Horn Publications, 1985.

_____. *The Custer Battle Casualties: Burials, Exhumations and Reinterments*. El Segundo, CA: Upton & Sons, 1989.

_____. *Lakota Recollections of the Custer Fight: New Sources of Indian-Military History*. Spokane: Arthur H. Clark Co., 1991.

_____. *Hokahey! A Good Day to Die! The Indian Casualties of the Custer Fight*. Spokane: Arthur H. Clark Co., 1993.

_____. *Cheyenne Memories: A Sourcebook*. Spokane: Arthur H. Clark Co., 1995.

_____. *Camp, Custer, and the Little Bighorn: A Collection of Walter Mason Camp's Research Papers on General George A. Custer's Last Fight*. El Segundo, CA: Upton & Sons, 1997.

_____. *The Surrender and Death of Crazy Horse: A Sourcebook about a Tragic Episode in Lakota History*. Spokane, WA: Arthur H. Clark Co., 1998.

_____. *The Custer Battle Casualties, II: The Dead, The Missing, and a Few Survivors*. El Segundo, CA: Upton & Sons, 1998.

_____. *On the Little Bighorn with Walter Camp*. El Segundo, CA: Upton & Sons, 2000.

_____. *Walter M. Camp's Little Bighorn Rosters*. Spokane, WA: Arthur H. Clark Co., 2002.

Hassrick, Royal B. *The Sioux: The Life and Customs of a Warrior Society*. Norman: University of Oklahoma Press, 1964.

Hyde, George E. *Red Cloud's Folk: A History of the Oglala Sioux Indians*. Norman: University of Oklahoma Press, 1937.

_____. *Life of George Bent*. Norman: University of Oklahoma Press, 1968.

Libby, Orin G. *The Arikara Narrative of the Campaign Against the Hostile Dakotas, June 1876*. New York: Sol Lewis, 1973.

Maine, Floyd Shuster. *Lone Eagle... The White Sioux*. Albuquerque: University of New Mexico Press, 1956.

Marquis, Thomas B. *Wooden Leg*. Lincoln: University of Nebraska Press, 1962.

_____. *Custer on the Little Bighorn*. Lodi, CA: End-Kian Publishing, 1971.

_____. *Cheyennes and Sioux*. Stockton, CA: University of Pacific Press, 1973.

_____. *Keep the Last Bullet for Yourself*. New York City: Two Continents Publishing Co., 1976.

Masters, Joseph G. *Shadows Fall Across the Little Horn: Custer's Last Stand*. Laramie: University of Wyoming Press, 1951.

McClernand, Edward J. *With the Indian and Buffalo in Montana, 1870–1878*. Glendale, CA: Arthur H. Clark Co., 1969.

McCreight, M. I. *Firewater and Forked Tongues*. Pasadena, CA: Trail's End Publishing, 1947.

McLaughlin, James. *My Friend the Indian*. Seattle: Superior Publishing, 1970.

Miles, Nelson A. *Personal Recollections and Observations of General Nelson A. Miles*. New York: Werner Co., 1897.

Olson, James C. *Red Cloud and the Sioux Problem*. Lincoln: University of Nebraska Press, 1965.

Powell, Peter J. and Michael P. Malone. *Montana, Past and Present*. Los Angeles: University of California Press, 1986.

Record of Engagements with Hostile Indians within the Mili-

tary Division of the Missouri from 1868 to 1882. Reprint. Fort Collins, CO: The Old Army Press, 1972.

Scott, Douglass D. and Richard A. Fox, Jr. *Archaeological Insights into the Custer Battle.* Norman: University of Oklahoma Press, 1987.

Standing Bear, Luther. *My People the Sioux.* Lincoln: University of Nebraska Press, 1975.

Stands in Timber and Margot Liberty. *Cheyenne Memories.* Lincoln: University of Nebraska Press, 1972.

Tassin, Ray. *Stanley Vestal, Champion of the Old West.* Glendale, CA: Arthur H. Clark Co., 1973.

Utley, Robert M., intro. *The Reno Court of Inquiry: The Chicago Times Account.* Fort Collins, CO: Old Army Press, 1972.

Vaughn, J. W. *Indian Fights.* Norman: University of Oklahoma Press, 1966.

Vestal, Stanley. *Sitting Bull, Champion of the Sioux.* Boston: Houghton Mifflin, 1932.

_____. *Warpath, The True Story of the Fighting Sioux, Told in a Biography of Chief White Bull.* Boston: Houghton Mifflin, 1934.

_____. *New Sources of Indian History.* Norman: University of Oklahoma Press, 1934.

_____. *Warpath and Council Fire.* New York: Random House, 1948.

Walker, Judson Elliott. *Campaigns of General Custer.* New York: Promontory Press, 1966.

Wheeler, Col. Homer S. *Buffalo Days.* Indianapolis: Bobbs-Merrill, 1925.

Yost, Nelly Snyder. *Boss Cowman: The Recollections of Ed Lemmon, 1857–1946.* Lincoln: University of Nebraska Press, 1969.

Printed Sources—Articles

Anderson, Harry H. "Cheyennes at the Little Big Horn: A Study of Statistics." *North Dakota History* (Spring, 1960).

Bradley, Lt. James H. "The Journal of." *Contributions to the Historical Society of Montana II* (1896).

Eastman, Charles H. "The Story of the Little Big Horn." *Chautauquan* (July, 1900).

————. "Rain-in-the-Face." *The Outlook* (October 27, 1906).

Garland, Hamlin. "General Custer's Last Fight as Seen by Two Moon." *McClure Magazine* (September, 1898).

Godfrey, Edward S. "Custer's Last Battle." *Century Magazine* (1892).

Graham, W. A. "Custer's Battle Flags." *The Westerners Brand Book, 1950.* Los Angeles Westerners, 1951.

Greene, Jerome A. "Evidence and the Custer Enigma: A Reconstruction of Indian-Military History." *The Westerners Trail Guide* (Kansas City) (March-June, 1973).

Hardorff, Richard G. "Custer's Trail to Wolf Mountains: A Reevaluation of Evidence." *Custer and His Times: Book Two.* Fort Worth: Little Bighorn Associates, 1984.

Hedren, Paul L. "Carbine Extraction Failure at the Little Big Horn: A New Examination." *Military Collector and Historian* (Summer, 1973).

Mallery, Garrick. "Picture-Writing of the American Indian." *The Fourth Annual Report of the Bureau of Ethnology.* Washington, D.C.: Government Printing Office, 1893.

Marshall, Robert A. "How Many Indians Were There?" *Research Review* (June, 1977).

Vestal, Stanley. "White Bull and One Bull—An Appreciation." *Westerners Brand Book* (Chicago) (October, 1947).

Newspapers

Billings (Montana) *Daily Gazette*, 1911.
Billings Gazette, 1926, 1927, 1961.
Bismarck (North Dakota) *Tribune*, 1876, 1877, 1966.
Chicago Tribune, 1877, 1879.
Chicago Inter Ocean, 1912.
Chicago Times, 1877.
Denver (Sioux Falls) *Argus Leader*, 1925.
Hardin (Montana) *Tribune*, 1923.
Leavenworth Times, 1881.

Index